Canoeing the Adirondacks with Nessmuk

Nessmuk.

Canoeing the Adirondacks with Nessmuk

The Adirondack Letters of George Washington Sears

Edited by
DAN BRENAN

with Revisions by
Robert L. Lyon and Hallie E. Bond

THE ADIRONDACK MUSEUM/SYRACUSE UNIVERSITY PRESS

First Edition 1993

06   9 8 7 6 5 4

All photographs are courtesy of the Adirondack Museum.

Except for revisions to chapters 1 and 2 and the foreword, this book was previously published as *The Adirondack Letters of George Washington Sears, Whose Pen Name Was "Nessmuk,"* edited by Dan Brenan and published by the Adirondack Museum.

The paper used in this publication meets the minimum requirements of American National Standard for Information Sciences—Permanence of Paper for Printed Library Materials, ANSI Z39.48-1984.∞™

This book was printed on 50-pound natural Phoenix Opaque recycled paper stock.

Library of Congress Cataloging-in-Publication Data

Sears, George Washington, 1821–1890.
    Canoeing the Adirondacks with Nessmuk : the Adirondack letters of
George Washington Sears / edited by Dan Brenan with revisions by
Robert L. Lyon and Hallie E. Bond.
        p.   cm.
    ISBN 0-8156-2594-4
    1. Canoes and canoeing—New York (State)—Adirondack
Mountains—Guidebooks.   2. Adirondack Mountains (N.Y.)—
Guidebooks.   3. Sears, George Washington, 1821–1890.
I. Brenan, Dan, d. 1962.   II. Title.
GV776.N72N347   1993
797.1'22'097475—dc20   93-16869

Manufactured in the United States of America

CONTENTS

DAN BRENAN, a writer of "angling literature," was born in Plattsburgh, New York, in 1885. He died in 1962, shortly before the original edition of this book was published.

ROBERT L. LYON is a retired journalist and art critic for the *Corning Leader*. A native of Wellsboro, Pennsylvania, he has been conducting research on Nessmuk for many years.

HALLIE E. BOND, curator of collections and boats at the Adirondack Museum, specializes in historic watercraft, including Adirondack guideboats and Rushton canoes. She curated the museum's permanent exhibit, "Boats and Boating in the Adirondacks," which opened in 1991.

PLATES

TABLE

FOREWORD

More than a century has passed since *Forest and Stream* first published a series of letters by the diminutive journalist and woodsman, George Washington Sears, describing his excursions by canoe along Adirondack waterways. Twenty-one years ago these letters appeared in book form, snatched from archival oblivion by Sears enthusiast Dan Brenan and published by the Adirondack Museum. Judging from the thickness of the original manuscript and Brenan's correspondence from 1959 to 1962 with the museum's director, Robert Bruce Inverarity, Brenan clearly intended the life and work of George Washington Sears (his "Nessmuk saga") to be his magnum opus. After its completion, however, the manuscript wandered in limbo until, with the help of Inverarity, its editing passed to Paul Jamieson, professor of English at St. Lawrence University, who focused only on Sears' Adirondack letters. At the same time his manuscript was being trimmed, Brenan's health was deteriorating. The exchange of letters between Inverarity and Brenan from 1961 on tell a poignant tale of a race with time, both men hoping fervently that Brenan would live to see his book in print. He did not. The book became mired at the printer, and Brenan died just weeks before its publication on August 31, 1962.

"The rescue of the Adirondack Letters of George Washington Sears," wrote Dan Brenan in the 1962 foreword, "is the purpose of this book. Nessmuk himself needs little introduction to the many outdoorsmen who still prize their copies of his *Woodcraft*, a manual that has gone through many printings since its first edition in

1884. . . . Of [Nessmuk's] ninety-odd contributions to *Forest and Stream* during the 1880's, the eighteen letters describing his three cruises in the Adirondacks are a natural choice. They form a consecutive narrative and give a lively, sharply-observant picture of the Adirondacks in the years 1880–1883."

Since Sears' *Adirondack Letters* went out of print in the early 1980's, there have been numerous requests for it. But there have also been problems. Robert L. Lyon, a journalist and native of Sears' hometown, Wellsboro, Pennsylvania, who knew the Sears family and who was writing his own biography of Sears, pointed out errors and inconsistencies in Brenan's account, arising perhaps from Brenan's failing health and the rush to put the book in print. Much of Brenan's information on Rushton had become outdated. When in 1992 Syracuse University Press invited the museum to reissue the book as a joint publication, we faced a dilemma: Should we feign ignorance and simply reprint it as it was or spend the money and time to revise the first two chapters? Or we could do nothing. But Nessmuk's reputation seemed indomitable; rescuing his words once again would be honorable and appropriate.

This revised edition corrects the biographical errors in chapter 1 and updates and adds new material to the section on J. H. Rushton. A few photographs, all now in the museum's permanent collection, have been substituted for those we could not find. Sears' letters are unchanged from Brenan's accurate transcriptions from *Forest and Stream*. The museum extends its special thanks to Robert L. Lyon for his willingness to correct misconceptions about Sears' life and for his invaluable help to set the record straight. We also thank Hallie E. Bond, curator of boats and collections at the museum, for her graceful complete revision of the second chapter. For a generous contribution toward the printing of this edition and recognition of Nessmuk as a Pennsylvanian "who made a difference," we thank Mary Sheffer and the board of the McInroy-Sheffer People Trust.

Dan Brenan gratefully acknowledged the following individuals for their help with the 1962 edition: Robert Bruce Inverarity and Paul D. Jamieson; Mrs. Mazie Sears Bodine, daughter of one of Nessmuk's brothers, Charles Sears; Mrs. Ruth Worthington of the Saranac Free Library; James Fynmore, photographer; Atwood Manley, author; A. Fred Saunders, past commodore of the American Canoe Association; E. R. Shumway, photographer, and Mrs. Mary V. Darrin of Wellsboro, Pennsylvania; Herbert R. Helms; Warder Cadbury; Austin S. Hogan; and Nick Drahos of the New York State Department of Conservation.

ALICE WOLF GILBORN

Blue Mountain Lake, New York
June 1993

Canoeing the Adirondacks with Nessmuk

NESSMUK HIMSELF

George Washington Sears was born at South Oxford, Massachusetts (now known as Webster), December 2, 1821. He was the eldest of ten children, seven boys and three girls. In the Preface to his volume of poems, *Forest Runes*, he tells of the origin of his pen name, Nessmuk. A young Indian whose tribal name was Nessmuk, meaning wood duck or wood drake in the Narragansett tongue, taught him the rudiments of woodcraft when he was a small boy. He never forgot the lessons in camping, fishing and hunting. In later years when he began writing for publication, he used the name as his own, in grateful memory of the Indian in whose company he enjoyed so many happy hours.

At age eight Sears was put to work in the cotton mill of Samuel Slater, a pioneer of the American Industrial

Revolution, and here he labored from early morning until dark. During mill shutdowns, Sears escaped to the woods and roamed them with his Indian friend. His prodigious reading helped make up for his lack of schooling. At twelve, the young Sears fled to Cape Cod, home of his grandmother, where, he tells us in one of his *Forest and Stream* letters, "it was my daily task to pull an oar (not a swivel oar, but loose in tholepins) from East Dennis, on the fishhook end of Cape Cod, straight out to sea, in a second-hand whaleboat, for fish."

Sears was nearly twenty before he fully succumbed to the salt water in his blood and signed on as a common sailor aboard the whaling ship *Rajah,* out of New Bedford, Mr. West, master. He was at sea in the Pacific for three years, from August 3, 1841, to July 17, 1844, as documented by his government shipping papers, preserved in the Melville Whaling Room of the New Bedford Free Public Library. Sea images from his voyage on a whaler would continually appear in Sears' later writings. In *Forest and Stream* for August 10, 1882, he reported: "In my young manhood I 'pulled stroke' in the waist boat of old *Rajah,* of and from New Bedford, West master." On September 2 of that same year, in the *American Angler,* he wrote again of his youthful experiences at sea. "In latitude 10 degrees north we catch a snorter from the S.W. . . . For 36 hours it is a sea fight for life, but at last we win. The perfect trim and full crew of the old *Rajah* pull us through. The gale subsides; the S.E. trades and regular swells prevail again, and the *Rajah* resumes her regular work—'cruisin' for sperm.' "

In what was perhaps intended to be a confidential letter

(undated) to the editor of *Forest and Stream*, published in May 1918, twenty-eight years after his death, Sears said:

> To myself I sometimes appear as a wild Indian or an old Berserker, masquerading under the guise of a nineteenth century American. When the strait jacket of civilization becomes too oppressive, I throw it off, betake myself to savagery, and there loaf and refresh my soul.
>
> I suppose I might be called tolerably well educated. Like Shakespeare, I have a little Latin and less Greek, know somewhat of the mysteries of the laboratory and microscope, while belles-lettres and literature are not totally unknown to me. . . .
>
> I love a horse, a gun, a dog, a trout and a pretty girl. I hate a pothunter, a trout-liar and a whiskey-guzzling sportsman. I smoke and take an occasional glass of wine and never lie about my hunting and fishing exploits more than the occasion seems to demand.

The Sears family moved from Massachusetts to Brockport, New York, in 1838, before young George went to sea, and where he returned after his voyage aboard the whaler to resume his father's trade of shoemaking. In 1848 the family moved to Wellsboro, Pennsylvania. This was to be his home for the remainder of his life when he wasn't adventuring in the wilderness areas of the Northwest or Brazil or the Adirondacks. In 1857 he married Mariette Butler who bore him three children, one son and two daughters. Mrs. Sears outlived Nessmuk by many years and died on December 4, 1925, at the age of ninety-three.

Sears' travels took him seven times to Michigan. On one of these trips, in company with one Charles Vance, he was on contract to supply meat to the work crew of a railroad then being built. A vivid description in *Woodcraft*, one of the highlights of his forest narratives, tells of a solitary trek across Michigan, from Saginaw Bay to the Muskegon River, when the region was practically a pathless wilderness. Between 1852 and 1853 he again traveled to Michigan with a companion, Ned Miller. Four letters published posthumously in *Forest and Stream* (December 11, 18 and 25, 1890, and January 1, 1891) describe the venture. The two men had planned to stay in Michigan all winter, hunting and camping, but Miller became homesick and lovesick, quarreled with Nessmuk, and packed up his duffel and went home. Nessmuk was left alone. He hunted, loafed, and generally enjoyed himself, for camping alone in the wilderness was the life he prized above all others. Then he became seriously ill, with the worst of the winter still to come. For days at a time he was hardly able to leave the shack, and the physical effort to chop enough wood to keep from freezing taxed his strength to the utmost. He was found by his own guide, a Chippewa Indian, who had returned to make a call. In the spring, at sugar season, he joined the band of Chippewas who nursed him back to health.

At the outbreak of the Civil War in 1861 President Lincoln issued a call for volunteers. Although thirty-nine years old, married, and the father of a growing family, Sears enlisted on May 31, 1861, in Company E, 13th Pennsylvania Reserves, 42nd of the Line, popularly known as the Bucktails. It is said that his regiment was made up of lumberjacks, woodsmen and hunters who were also sharpshooters. Sears served until he was discharged three months later with the rank of sergeant, on August 2, 1861, after being hospitalized twice for asthma.

In the fall of 1866 Sears and his brother Charles made

a trip to Minnesota for the purpose of trapping. They passed through "the village of New Lisbon, on the Lemonweir River, Wisconsin," to visit relatives (Sears' sister-in-law) and returned to Wellsboro on New Year's Day, 1867. Not long after, the lure of far places led him to Brazil. While there he investigated the crude rubber industry, Brazil's major industry at that time. He was certain that he could improve the method of drying the latex, the liquid sap of the rubber tree. He tried to interest the government officials in his method, but they were slow to respond. While waiting for them to take action, he made a long journey up the Amazon River by steamboat, continuing up one of the tributaries in a smaller craft. Louis Agassiz, the famous naturalist, had made the same journey the previous year, and Nessmuk had a copy of Agassiz's printed account with him. Back in Wellsboro in September 1867, he interested potential investors in his rubber scheme. But a second trip to Brazil in 1870 ended in failure to persuade authorities to consider his plan.

In his first letter to *Forest and Stream* Nessmuk says that "I dropped the pen in '71." He resigned from the *Tioga County Agitator*, of which he had been editor, on October 28, 1871, and wrote no more prose for publication until *Forest and Stream* began to publish his letters in 1880. The eighteen letters in this book describe Sears' canoe cruises in the Adirondacks from July 1880 through August 1883.

After the Adirondack cruise of 1883 in *Sairy Gamp*, Sears returned to Wellsboro where he wrote the text for his classic *Woodcraft*. Published by the Forest and Stream Publishing Company in 1884 and one of the first works of its kind in America, it covers practically the entire field of contemporary outdoor life—camping, hunting, fishing, camp cooking, canoeing and other subjects. The book has remained popular for nearly a century and was reprinted in paperback as late as 1963.

In 1883 Nessmuk was invited to contribute a chapter to Charles F. Orvis and A. Nelson Cheney's book, *Fishing with the Fly*. He accepted. This work is a symposium, with chapters by twenty-four well-known angling writers of the period, including Charles Hallock, George Dawson, Henry P. Wells, James A. Henshall, Seth Green, Fred Mather and others. Nessmuk's chapter, entitled "Trout; Meeting Them on the June Rise," makes a feeble attempt to justify his pretensions as a fly-fisher by giving his dressings for several standard fly patterns. The perfunctory effort may not have convinced even Nessmuk himself. The chapter is totally lacking in the spirited, self-assured style characteristic of his best prose, the kind he wrote when he knew what he was walking about. Fred Mather, in *My Angling Friends*, belittles his skill in fly-fishing. The significant point to us, however, is the fact that in 1883 Nessmuk had earned so high a reputation as to merit the invitation. His co-authors were certainly the elite of the angling writers of that era.

Nessmuk remained in Wellsboro almost a year and a half, alarmed by failing health. He sought relief from the severe northern winters in 1885 by accepting an invitation to go to Florida from one of his admirers, Captain S. D. Kendall, a retired sea captain who contributed to *Forest and Stream* under the pen name "Tarpon." In May 1886 he returned to Wellsboro. He had contracted a severe attack of malaria in Florida, and this added affliction caused him to write, in the fall of 1886: "Looking from my window out on the bleak hillside where the snow lies in rugged patches on the damp, dark plowed ground, my soul hungers for the pleasant camp at the head of Lake Butler or the larger, better appointed camp where I kept my traps and made my headquarters for more than a twelvemonth at the Oak and Pine."

Relief came once again in the form of an invitation to become one of a crew of five members to go to Florida aboard a private yacht, the *Stella*. The vessel left New York on Christmas morning, 1886, and reached the east coast of Florida after several exciting experiences. Nessmuk left the party and went ashore, setting up camp on a tributary of the Halifax River. He fished, loafed and hunted. Quail and wild turkey were plentiful, although he suffered some twinges of conscience when hunting quail. "I always felt a little ashamed of murdering such cute, beautiful things for a few ounces of meat; knowing in my conscience that hog and hominy were quite as good fare as I deserved," he wrote in one of seven letters to *Forest and Stream* describing his second Florida trip.

Sears reluctantly broke camp April 6, 1887, when the time came for him to rejoin the crew of the *Stella*, as had been agreed. This was to be the last of his camping trips. His health deteriorated rapidly from that time to the early months of 1890.

In his diary entry of January 5, 1881, Nessmuk wrote that he had started to make up a manuscript of poems the month before. He subsequently sent the completed manuscript, called *Forest Runes*, to *Forest and Stream* where it languished until 1886 when the editors decided to publish it. The book was printed and ready for distribution in March 1887. It contains eighty-five original poems, including the dedicatory verse to Nessmuk's brother Charles, twenty-one of which may be classified as poems of the forest. The remaining poems embrace a medley of subjects ranging from somber philosophical musings to light comedy, not unmixed with ribaldry. The book has never been republished and copies are now quite scarce. As to its literary merit, perhaps that subject had best be left to the "sparrow-hawks of criticism," whose generous indulgence he hoped for in his Preface.

Particular mention should be made of Nessmuk's many letters pleading for better sportsmanship and observance of laws designed to help conserve our dwindling wild game and fish. In his later years he became what might be termed a fanatic on the subject; he attacked the game-hogs with fiery vigor. It may have appeared a thankless and hopeless cause to him in his time, but if he and the other pioneers of conservation and good sportsmanship could return now, they would find their reward in the realization that their teachings have not been in vain.

His critics have passed away. But Nessmuk still appeals to a wide audience, and he lives on especially in the hearts and thoughts of woodsmen and sportsmen through kinship in the written word. His name stands as high with them as the rugged Mount Nessmuk that presides over Marsh Creek, near Wellsboro, where he lived, camped, fished and hunted.

After the second trip to Florida the few outings Nessmuk enjoyed in the next two years were limited to his home neighborhood, and even these grew shorter and less frequent as the months went by. Malaria and pulmonary trouble were taking their toll. The news of his serious illness reached his friends and well-wishers throughout the country. He received many invitations to visit friends who sympathized with his plight and offered what help they could. To all of these he sent his sincere thanks, but none could be accepted.

One of his letters of thanks, published posthumously, is particularly pathetic. It was written to one of his friends, Captain L. A. Beardslee, then in command of the battleship *Vermont*. The Captain, a frequent contributor to *Forest and Stream* under the pen name "Piseco," had urged Nessmuk to visit him aboard the *Vermont*, pointing out the advantages of skilled medical care, the benefit of sea air, and the stimulation of unfamiliar scenes and places to revive his zest in life. Nessmuk replied from Wellsboro:

> Your letter was a long time on the road, but it came safe at last and I was glad to hear from you once more. It found me on the invalid list and unable to hunt, canoe or fish. I seldom get beyond the front yard, and the gun is of no further use to me, while I have not put the old rod together in two years. Time and "physical disability" will . . . beat every mother's son of us and I do not complain. Few men have had as much of life in the woods as I have, and memory at least can not be taken away from me while my senses hold good.
>
> I would like of all things to report on board the old Vermont for an old-time visit, but it doesn't lay in the pins, more's the pity. Ah me! how vividly I recall the visit, all too short, that we had at Moose River years ago. *Tempus fugit.* Let him fly; let him flicker. I have been there, and done it; and if I were young again I would do it some more.
>
> No. I have not written much for the press in the last year or so. I can not get over the inane listlessness and laziness induced by a long, tedious siege of malaria, and it seems as though the old-time energy and vim would never return. I have lost all ambition.
>
> I have seen very little from your pen lately, for which I

am sorry. Your articles on the salmon of the Northwest Coast were most excellent and instructive, the best ever written on the subject, and you always interest me, anyhow.

Just now our forests are in the best color, and you know what that means. It is my favorite time of year, the time of fruition and beauty, also of deer hunting, with grouse hunting, etc. Ah, *culpa mea!* Shall be pleased to hear from you again, and will always answer. And if I were in better condition I would write a better epistle. But this will do to convey the sincere regards of "Nessmuk."

George W. Sears

In the spring of 1890 Nessmuk was so enfeebled that he was unable to leave the house without help. As a last reminder of his many forest campfires of happier years, the family set up his tent and camping duffel in the yard, and there he made believe at camping with his grandchildren.

At early dawn on May 1, 1890, he passed peacefully away.

The funeral was held the following Saturday, and friends from far and near gathered to pay a last tribute. The casket was carried to the little grove of hemlocks in front of the house, the grove he writes of in his poem "My Attic":

And trees, not standing in stiff, straight rows,
All planted and pruned by the owner's hand,
Lovingly tended, thriftily grown,
With many a quaint, odd crook and trend—
I know their names as I know my own,
And every tree is a personal friend.

He was buried there among the hemlocks. Messages came from all parts of the country. Boy Scout Troops were named in his honor; fish and game clubs perpetuated his name; a mountain in northern Pennsylvania was named Mount Nessmuk by the State Geographic Board; and half a mile above the site of Nessmuk's home, Lake Nessmuk was named in his memory. James Whitcomb Riley offered a tribute in verse.

It was inevitable that someone would suggest a fitting memorial, and *Forest and Stream* immediately offered to act as custodian of subscriptions and trustee of the project. George W. Brewster, the artist and sculptor, offered to design and cast a bronze tablet in bas-relief. Friends in Wellsboro offered to provide a suitable base. Both offers were accepted and subscriptions were received in ample amount.

The memorial was not erected immediately. Late in 1892 the casket was removed to the village cemetery. In 1893 the memorial was placed over Nessmuk's grave with a simple ceremony of dedication. There it stands today, a shrine for those who revere the memory of the woodsman who lies beneath it.

"THE FEATHER WEIGHT
AND THE BACKWOODS"

From his home in Wellsboro, on June 9, 1880, George Washington Sears informed the editor of *Forest and Stream* that he was planning a trip to the Adirondacks.

> My canoe is ready for launching. She is clinker built, of white cedar, and the lightest that ever went through the Adirondacks. Weight, seventeen pounds, thirteen and three-quarters ounces. If I live a month longer, there will be another "fool i' the forest." The "melancholy Jacques" may find him somewhere between the Fulton Chain and the lower waters of the West St. Regis, drowned, with a capsized cockleshell nearby.
>
> For I am going through alone. . . .
>
> There are five thousand pleasant, shady nooks in the Northern Wilderness on which a camp was never raised. Colvin's Report shows that the heart-cores of the Wilderness are as yet

unexplored. His final map will show not less than three hundred new lakes and ponds never before mapped.

I have traveled in foreign lands; have been twice to the Amazon Valley; and I rise to remark that there is but one Adirondack Wilderness on the face of the earth. And, if the great State of New York fails to see and preserve its glorious gifts, future generations will have cause to curse and despise the petty, narrow greed that converts into saw-logs and mill-dams the best gifts of wood and water, forest and stream, mountains and crystal springs in deep wooded valleys that the sun shines on at this day.

Nessmuk's subsequent Adirondack letters were avidly read. By his death in 1890, they had helped promote both the "North Woods" and his canoe builder, J. H. Rushton, who by then was acknowledged as one of the premier boat builders in the country. The letters also helped focus public attention on issues of game conservation and wilderness preservation. But Nessmuk's Adirondack correspondence also has significance for the historian and the canoeist one hundred years later. "Going through alone," without the services of a professional guide, was a revolutionary concept in 1880. The craft which made possible solo traveling, Nessmuk's "clinker-built cockle-shell," was new at the time as well. Both have since become standard as ways of enjoying the wilderness.

Nessmuk's reasons for visiting the wilderness would not seem unusual today. Nessmuk and his contemporaries felt that a sojourn in the woods could provide an antidote to the pollution and crime of the newly industrialized cities. Nessmuk was only one of many observers who explained the lure of the wilderness when he wrote in one of his "forest runes":

For brick and mortar breed filth and crime,
With a pulse of evil that throbs and beats;

. . . .

And death stalks in on the struggling crowd—
But he shuns the shadow of oak and pine.

The salubrious life in the shadows of the Adirondack
pines had been described by several widely read writers
by Nessmuk's time. Joel Tyler Headley's *The Adirondack,
or Life in the Woods* (1849) and Samuel H. Hammond's
Wild Northern Scenes (1857) were just two. The most
popular book on the subject, however, was written by a
Boston clergyman named William Henry Harrison
Murray and appeared shortly after the close of the Civil
War. *Adventures in the Wilderness* was an instant success.
So alluring was Murray's image of outdoors life, his book
actually started a "rush" to the wilderness. Patronage of
the Raquette Lake House, just one hostelry in the center
of the woods, doubled the summer the book appeared.
The impact of the book may have been even greater on
the fringes of the wilderness.[1]

A great deal of the popularity of Murray's book had to
do with the picture he painted of the ease of woods travel.
"There is nothing in the journey that the most delicate
and fragile need fear," he wrote, trying to allay the fears
of lady campers.[2] By 1869, when the book first appeared,
the rough pioneer stage of Adirondack transportation had
passed. Railroads, steamboats and stagecoaches made
travel to the region cheap and relatively comfortable.
Once there, a large population of knowledgeable, professional guides made it easy to get around. One didn't even
need to camp out, for hotels large and small offered the

casual tourist a taste of the wilderness from a comfortable setting.

In Nessmuk's day most visitors to the Adirondacks saw the region from the stern seat of an Adirondack guideboat rowed by a professional guide. Guideboats are flat-bottomed rowing boats with sawn frames, first cousins to the ocean-going dory and descendants of the bateaux used by the British in the colonial wars.[3] They are unique to the region and were developed by early settlers who needed a fast, capacious boat which could also be carried over the many portages in the region. The standard guideboat of Murray's day was from fifteen to sixteen feet long and weighed around seventy-five pounds. It was carried by means of a yoke like that used to carry sap or water buckets.

The availability of guides with guideboats to row through the region's marvelous network of waterways did make visiting the Adirondack's relatively easy, but a guide was expensive. The average workman who built Nessmuk's boat made fifteen cents per hour.[4] A barrel of flour, a staple of life, cost about two-thirds of a week's wages.[5] According to Murray, the cost of hiring a guide and his boat was $2.50 per day plus board, which was beyond the reach of craftsmen and clerks.[6]

The sometime shoemaker Nessmuk had firsthand experience with the budgets of craftsmen, but he felt that they needed a restorative vacation in the woods just as much as wealthier visitors. It was possible, he argued, *if* one could dispense with the guide. All one really needed was a means of finding one's way, a familiarity with woodcraft, and a light, easily managed boat.

By 1880, the year of Nessmuk's first Adirondack trip,

the main routes through the woods were easily found. On the most popular tours the carries were marked and, as Nessmuk tells us in several of his letters, up-to-date information could be acquired from fellow travelers. Perhaps most importantly, good maps were available. These accurate, available maps were due in large part to the work of Verplanck Colvin, to whom Nessmuk referred in his first letter to *Forest and Stream,* quoted above.

Colvin is famous today because his survey reports published almost yearly from 1872 through 1900 read like adventure stories and because he was of the early advocates of the Adirondack Park's creation. But often overlooked was his background as a professional surveyor. By 1880, in large part because of Colvin's work, Seneca Ray Stoddard and E. R. Wallace vied with each other yearly to produce maps for the masses. Their maps accompanied guidebooks containing information on accommodations, the characters of villages in the region, guides and a wealth of important information for the tourist.

Nessmuk wrote his 1884 volume *Woodcraft* to provide the novice with a knowledge of woodcraft, "the rod, rifle, canoe, camp, and in short the entire list of forest lore and backwoods knowledge,"[7] which he would need to "go through alone." The guiding principle in *Woodcraft* was to "go light, the lighter the better, so that you have the simplest material for health, comfort and enjoyment."[8] It was certainly enjoyable for anyone, then as now, to "go light," but for Nessmuk it was physically imperative. Entering his sixties at the time of his Adirondack cruises, weighing about 105 pounds, and probably suffering from tuberculosis, Nessmuk found the longer carries exhausting, as he tells us in several of his letters (see pp.

78–79, 117, and 132). His heaviest Adirondack canoe weighed less than eighteen pounds, yet the task of getting it across the carries sometimes taxed his strength to the utmost.

The most important piece of gear for a solo trip through the Adirondacks, "whose Highways are rivers, whose paths are streams,"[9] was a light boat. The Adirondack guideboat was light for a sixteen-foot skiff but was too fragile, expensive and cranky for a novice. Nessmuk went shopping for a new type of craft, and he settled on a canoe—but not the canoe paddled by most of his contemporaries and not the birchbark of the natives who had paddled the waters of the Adirondacks for centuries.

The dawn of a golden age in American canoeing and canoe building occurred in 1880. Not only was it the year that Nessmuk paddled his first Rushton canoe but it was also the year of the founding of the American Canoe Association on Lake George. Modern canoeing was a popular sport, and there were canoe builders throughout the Northeast and eastern Canada from whom Nessmuk could buy a boat. James Everson, William P. Stephens, W. Jarvis and George Roahr, all in New York State, were well known because they advertised nationally or were mentioned in introductory canoeing texts. Further afield was a group of builders of open canoes in the Peterborough area north of Toronto. Close to the area Nessmuk planned to explore were H. M. Sprague in Parishville and J. H. Rushton in Canton.[10]

Most canoe builders of 1880 concentrated on the modern decked sailing canoe which had come into vogue after the Civil War. As Rushton himself put it in a letter to Nessmuk, "you like the feather weight and the backwoods. So do I . . . *but* as a matter of business and to make the builder known abroad the *decked* sailing canoes are the ones I have to look after."[11] The sailing canoe was developed in England in the late 1850's on the model of the Inuit kayak and within thirty years had evolved into a tiny yacht complete with mainsail and mizzen.

Nessmuk was not interested in the decked sailing canoe. With its deck and rig, it was too heavy to carry over the many portages in the Adirondacks. He found a craft which better suited his needs in the catalog of J. H. Rushton.

John Henry Rushton was born near Edwards, in the northern foothills of the Adirondacks, in 1843. He and Nessmuk were remarkably alike, both physically and in their love for the woods. Both were small men. Rushton stood just a hair over five feet tall and weighed "111½ when *feeling well*."[12] Nessmuk was five feet three inches tall and weighed around 110 pounds. Rushton seems to have been more of a family man than Nessmuk; in 1884 he remarked to Nessmuk, "I *love* my business next to my wife and the wild woods."[13] The story of each is incomplete without that of the other. Nessmuk could not have cruised the Adirondacks as he did—and been such an eager proponent of the "go-light" philosophy—without a light boat. By the same token, Rushton's early fame was due in large part to the publicity he received through the Adirondack letters of George Washington Sears.

At the age of thirty Rushton began building "portable boats" of "extreme lightness" in Canton, not far from his boyhood home. By 1880 he was building sailing canoes and several other types of pleasure craft, but he also offered unusually short, open "hunting canoes." Many of

Nessmuk's contemporaries must have wondered at the utility of eleven- and twelve-foot-long boats when most builders built no shorter than fourteen feet, but Nessmuk was intrigued.

The small hunting canoe of the type offered by Rushton probably has as long a pedigree in the Adirondacks as the more famous Adirondack guideboat. Rushton himself described the type of boat carrying two people he had used in the 1850's in the northern Adirondacks as "a light open boat or canoe 11 to 13 feet long, 30 to 36 inches wide and weighing from 25 to 50 pounds." [14] The boats were probably lapstrake and built up off a keel, descendants of the lapstrake skiffs built and used by the British settlers in the St. Lawrence valley to the north. [15]

Nessmuk made one significant departure from the canoe tradition of Rushton's childhood. Instead of a single-bladed paddle, he used a double blade for most of his paddling. Nessmuk probably adopted this from the cruising canoeists, who in turn had taken up the paddle of the Inuit, whose boat they adapted.

In his concern for lightness Rushton revealed his Adirondack background. Like the early guideboat builders, he aimed to make his hunting boats light enough to carry easily from waterway to waterway. "It is wonderful how few pounds of cedar, rightly modeled and properly put together, it takes to float a man," he once wrote to Nessmuk. [16] His "system" for combining lightness and strength, which he used in all his boats, was unusual in its day. He pared down the weight by using thin planking and ribs, and then recovered strength by placing the ribs close together. His early ribs were thin, flat strips of red elm, but early in the 1880's he began using half-round

ribs. Created by splitting a dowel, they were more com-
plicated to make than conventional ribs, but they supplied
greater strength for their weight than flat ribs of the same
weight. Rushton also boasted that he shaped every plank
to fit, rather than forcing it into place, which meant that
his boats had less tendency to go out of shape.

Nessmuk's business was a golden opportunity for
Rushton. Rushton had pioneered modern business prac-
tices such as cost accounting and national marketing
through catalogs and advertising, and he appreciated
Nessmuk providing him with advertisement of the very
best kind, free, unsolicited, and widespread.[17] He also
realized the value of testing his theories of boatbuilding
on a public stage. As he wrote to Nessmuk after his first
trial of *Sairy Gamp*, *"this shows what can be done by this
system of construction. I know it cannot be attained by any
other. If it cannot, then a 40 or 50 or 100 # boat built on
the same system must be stronger than one of equal weight*
built in some other manner. That is my position—*you*
pay your money and take your choice. . . . By so doing
advertise me as a builder and *that* is so much *cash* to
me."[18]

Rushton built five boats for Nessmuk within six years.
Nessmuk claimed to be delighted with each one, but he
kept ordering new ones. It seems to have become an on-
going challenge for Rushton and Nessmuk to develop the
perfect small canoe (see table). Rushton probably also
offered Nessmuk incentives to continue the quest because
it was so good for business. Although Rushton warned
Nessmuk in 1880, "if in the first place you had proposed
that I *give* you a canoe for 'blowing' I should have said *no
sir.*"[19] *Sairy Gamp* cost Nessmuk only twenty dollars in

1882, when Rushton's Nessmuk models, only six inches longer, cost ordinary customers ten dollars more.

Rushton Boats Used by Nessmuk

Year	Name	Length (feet)	Beam (inches)	Depth at center (inches)	Weight[a]
1880	*Nessmuk*[b]	10	26	8	17 lbs. 9½ oz.
1881	*Susan Nipper*[c]	10½	28	8	16 lbs.
1882	*Sairy Gamp*	9	26	6	10½ lbs.
1884	*Bucktail*[d]	10½	26	9	22 lbs.
1885	*Rushton*[e]	8½	23	8	9 lbs. 15 oz.

[a] Nessmuk is not always consistent in stating the weights of his boats. Heavier weights may have resulted from added thwarts or paint over the life of the boat, not to mention inaccurate measurement. In this table the lightest weights are given.

[b] Also called *Wood Drake* in Sears, *Forest and Stream*, Aug. 12, 1880, 34. Nessmuk calls it *Nessmuk*, at 17 pounds, 13¾ ounces, in an article about his boats (Sears, *Forest and Stream*, Dec. 3, 1885, 574).

[c] Listed as 16 pounds in Sears, *Forest and Stream*, Dec. 3, 1885, 374, and 16 pounds, 9 ounces, in Sears, *Forest and Stream*, Oct. 23, 1884, 242.

[d] *Bucktail* is the boat Nessmuk had just ordered as he published *Woodcraft* in 1884. It was to be "on lines and dimensions that, in my judgement, will be found nearly perfect for the average canoeist of 150–160 pounds." (*Woodcraft*, 13th ed., 135–36). Listed as 24 pounds in other sources (Sears, *Forest and Stream*, Oct. 2, 1884, 183, and Dec. 3, 1885, 374).

[e] Sears, *Forest and Stream*, July 16, 1885, 486.

Nessmuk's first boat was known variously as *Nessmuk* and *Wood Drake*. She was used for the 1880 cruise only and was sold in 1881 to Bob Perrie, a guide and proprietor of a public camp on Third Lake, Fulton Chain.

Susan Nipper, named after a character in Dickens's

Dombey and Son, was used only for the 1881 cruise. Sears had planned to take her on a cruise in 1882 but was prevented by ill health. He kept the boat at least until 1884, when he took her down the Susquehanna, after which she was "racked and leaky." *Susan Nipper* had a "light carrying frame . . . but she is very frail, scarcely fit for river work," wrote Sears.[20]

Sairy Gamp was ordered for the 1883 cruise. She is the best documented of the boats, and the only one to survive. In late 1882 Nessmuk's health was failing, but he planned one last Adirondack cruise. In November Rushton finished this third boat for the old woodsman. Notice of the order had appeared in *Forest and Stream,* and Rushton thought "I had best build that canoe as some one might inquire after it."[21] When finished, the boat was only nine feet long and weighed ten-and-a-half pounds. She was supposedly named for the tippling nurse in Dickens's *Martin Chuzzlewit* who "took no water." Rushton was justifiably proud of his work but regarded it primarily as an experiment. "Now you must *stop* with *this* one," he wrote to Nessmuk. "Don't try any smaller one. If you get sick of this as a *Canoe,* use it for a soup dish."[22]

Rushton couldn't resist a test run in *Sairy Gamp* when she was finished in early November. After weighing the boat, he "took her to the river, put on rubbers, laid a strip of 1/4 in. cedar in the bottom and got into her ([I weigh] 108#). She closed together an inch or more on top and I did not know but she would collapse. After *feeling* of her, shaking her a little, I paddled off. Steady enough, *four inches out* of water amidship—only *one* danger, 'frailty.' Still, *every piece* is *selected* with *care* and she *may shake* a good deal without *breaking.*"[23] Nessmuk found the canoe satisfactory as well. She only dumped him once in his six-week cruise, and that, he admits, was through his own carelessness.

Nessmuk sent *Sairy Gamp* back to Rushton after the 1883 cruise. Rushton then sent the boat to New York, where she was exhibited in the *Forest and Stream* office. In 1884 she was sent to the Cotton Exposition in New Orleans. Her history from that date to 1893, when she was exhibited in the *Forest and Stream* booth at the Columbian Exposition at Chicago, is obscure. She now belongs to the Smithsonian Institution and is on permanent loan to the Adirondack Museum.

Nessmuk never returned to the Adirondacks after the cruise of the *Sairy Gamp*. He ordered two further boats from Rushton which he used in Pennsylvania and Florida. The fourth canoe, *Bucktail,* was a return to a more practical craft. "As an open twenty-four pound canoe I don't see how she can be improved; and she is able and lively with a freight of 225 pounds," Nessmuk wrote.[24] The boat was named after Nessmuk's Civil War regiment and was sold to a Commodore Phinney in Florida.

Even though Rushton warned Nessmuk not to order any smaller boats than *Sairy Gamp,* the final canoe he built for the woodsman actually was smaller than *Sairy Gamp.* The *Rushton* was named in part "as a slight compliment to the man who has done more and better canoe work for me than any man living."[25] Nessmuk was delighted with her performance in sheltered waters in Florida but would not take her into conditions encountered in the Adirondacks a half-decade earlier.

Despite Rushton's misgivings about the practicality of the tiny canoes, Nessmuk's boats captured the popular imagination. By 1886 Rushton was bothered by all sorts of unrealistic expectations of the boats. "The trouble is," he wrote Nessmuk, "every d--- fool who weighs less than 300 thinks *he* can use such a canoe too. I get letters asking if the Bucktail will carry two good-sized men and camp duffel and be steady enough to stand up in and shoot out of. I told one fellow that I thought he'd shoot *out* of it mighty quick if he tried it."[26] One such "d--- fool" was William West Durant, the central Adirondack land developer. "He is near six ft. and 170# (guess)," wrote Rushton of Durant when Durant visited the shop during construction of *Sairy Gamp*. "I had hard work to keep him from ordering a duplicate, as it was he ordered a 'Nessmuk.' "[27] Durant named his boat, built on the dimensions of *Susan Nipper, Wee Lassie,* and it too is in the collections of the Adirondack Museum.

Although Rushton himself preferred a larger canoe, he was quick to recognize the appeal of Nessmuk's boats. The Nessmuk models were so popular they were carried in the Rushton catalogs until the shop closed during the First World War. Two generations later, small solo canoes had regained popularity. The Old Town Canoe Company began producing a fiberglass Nessmuk model in 1960, and by the centennial of the cruise of the *Susan Nipper, Wee Lassie* had become a generic term for a small "pack canoe." Countless pack canoes have since been made, in traditional construction, strip-built, fiberglass and Kevlar. Often shape or dimensions are altered a bit to suit either customers or materials, but the idea of the small solo canoe originated with J. H. Rushton and his most famous customer, a small solo canoeist whose pen name was Nessmuk.

With his letter from Wellsboro, Nessmuk established a relationship with *Forest and Stream* which was to last until the woodsman's death and be of great benefit to both. *Forest and Stream*, established in 1873 by Charles Hallock, was by 1880 the preeminent outdoors journal of the period. Over the next ten years, Nessmuk contributed more than ninety letters and articles containing about 250,000 words to the magazine. They vary in length from a few paragraphs to over five thousand words. They did not appear with any regularity. Often intervals of several months elapsed between letters. At other times Nessmuk wrote almost weekly, usually when he was at the center of some controversy.

Nessmuk became one of the magazine's most influential contributors. For more than a quarter-century, *Forest and Stream* held undisputed leadership in its field, and Nessmuk was an important factor in contributing to this success. The advantages were reciprocal. The magazine gave Nessmuk an opportunity to cultivate a following. In return he helped expand *Forest and Stream*'s readership. The periodical had originally featured primarily field sports; Nessmuk was perhaps the best-known of its writers to concentrate on wilderness travel for its own sake, although, of course, he did his share of hunting and fishing.

After reintroducing himself to the readers of *Forest and Stream* with his letter from Wellsboro, Nessmuk went by railroad to Boonville, New York, and there hired a "rig" to take him to Moose River settlement, a few miles north.

At Moose River he began the first series of six letters that describe his long anticipated adventure.

Many of the letters were written in the field after the day's journey was over. They were extemporary notes, jotted down with little attention to form or literary polish. Others were written after his return to Wellsboro. Of the six letters describing the first cruise in 1880, entitled "Rough Notes from the Woods," four were written at the Fulton Chain or elsewhere and two after the return to Wellsboro. They are vibrant with enthusiasm. Nessmuk had discovered a new world, the world promised by Verplanck Colvin, and he was eager to tell about it.

The four letters relating to the *Susan Nipper* cruise of 1881 were written after he had abandoned his plans of a long summer's cruise and returned home, ill and disconsolate. Somber in tone and tempered by his failing health, they give us a somewhat reserved portrayal of his experiences of that summer. They are more careful in composition, but the buoyant vigor and enthusiasm of the 1880 letters are lacking.

Nessmuk spent the summer of 1882 at home. He was too ill to venture far afield. He took as cheerful a view as possible of what must have been a bitter disappointment; for he had confidently planned another Adirondack cruise for the 1882 season. Perhaps anticipation of the next year's cruise sustained him.

The eight letters of the *Sairy Gamp* cruise of 1883 deserve special comment, for they were written when Nessmuk found himself at the pinnacle of his popularity and influence. The news of his coming spread through the mountains and up and down the waterways. Everyone wanted to see the miniature craft and its famous owner. He was invited to private camps, interviewed, questioned and photographed. The Nessmuk story spread far beyond the limits of *Forest and Stream*'s circulation; the public press, sensing a news story of more than usual human interest, gave full publicity to the third cruise. Nessmuk made the most of the social opportunities his new fame gave him, and he gave Murray, Stoddard and Wallace some competition in writing with authority about guides, hotel keepers, tourists and camp owners.

In vivid detail the pageantry of the waterways from a bygone era unfolds in the letters of Nessmuk's Adirondack voyages. These letters also popularize the craft which has become known as the "pack canoe" throughout North America. Most importantly, they document a significant stage in the development of tourism in the Adirondacks. In urging campers to "go through alone," Nessmuk furthered the democratization of wilderness travel, a trend which has benefited millions of "outers" since his time.

NOTES

1. William H. H. Murray, *Adventures in the Wilderness*, ed. William K. Verner (Syracuse: Adirondack Museum and Syracuse Univ. Press, 1970), 50. The calculations are from Warder H. Cadbury's introduction.

2. Ibid., 19.

3. For the complete story of the development of the Adirondack guideboat, see Kenneth and Helen Durant, *The Adirondack Guide-Boat* (Camden, Maine: International Marine Publ., and the Adirondack Museum, 1980). For more recent scholarship on the origins of the guideboat, see John Gardner, *The Dory Book* (Mystic, Conn.: Mystic Seaport Museum, 1987).

4. This is the rate in Rushton's shop for the mid-nineties, the only

years for which data are available ("Knowledge," MSS, shop notebooks, ca. 1895; Adirondack Museum Library). A ten-hour day is assumed. Judging from the pricing of Rushton's boats and what is known of the national economy at the time, wages were probably somewhat less in 1890 than in 1880.

5. Dorothy Brady, "Relative Prices in the Nineteenth Century," *Journal of Economic History* 24 (June 1964), 145–203.

6. Murray, *Adventures in the Wilderness*, 25.

7. George Washington Sears, *Forest and Stream*, July 8, 1880, 451.

8. George Washington Sears, *Woodcraft*, 13th ed. (New York: Forest and Stream Publ., 1918), 4.

9. Attributed to W. H. H. "Adirondack" Murray in *Paul Smith's Adirondack Park* (Troy, N.Y.: Troy Times Press, 1904), from the Adirondack Museum Library.

10. The builders listed are only the more prominent ones who advertised nationally. Nessmuk may have read the appendix to a popular canoeing book, C. L. Norton and John Habberton, *Canoeing in Kanuckia, or, Haps and Mishaps Afloat and Ashore* (New York: Putnam, 1878), which listed all the builders mentioned except Stephens and Sprague.

11. J. H. Ruston to George Washington Sears, Sept. 14, 1884, MSS 78.2, Adirondack Museum Library.

12. Ibid., May 2, 1880.

13. Ibid., Apr. 25, 1884.

14. J. H. Rushton, "Single vs. Double Blades," *American Canoeist*, July 1882, 93.

15. Philip Gillesse to Hallie Bond, Mar. 20, 1990, curatorial research files, Adirondack Museum.

16. Sears, *Woodcraft*, 133.

17. Tom Tyson, "The Nature and Function of Cost Keeping in a Late Nineteenth-Century Small Business," typescript, 1988, Adirondack Museum Library.

18. Rushton to Sears, Nov. 8, 1882.

19. Ibid.

20. Sears, "Log of the Bucktail," *Forest and Stream*, Oct. 23, 1884, 243.

21. Rushton to Sears, Nov. 1, 1882.

22. Ibid.

23. Rushton to Sears, Nov. 1, 1882.

24. Sears, *Forest and Stream,* Dec. 3, 1885, 374.
25. Sears, *Forest and Stream,* July 16, 1885, 486.
26. Rushton to Sears, Apr. 7, 1886.
27. Rushton to Sears, Nov. 23, 1882.

III

NESSMUK'S ADIRONDACK LETTERS

Moose River, July 21 (*F&S*, Aug. 12, 1880)

ROUGH NOTES from the WOODS She's all my fancy painted her, she's lovely, she is light. She waltzes on the waves by day and rests with me at night. But I had nothing to do with her painting. The man who built her did that. And I commence with the canoe because that is about the first thing you need on entering the Northern Wilderness. From the Forge House, foot of the Fulton Chain, on the west, to Paul Smith's, Lower St. Regis Lake, on the east, is ninety-two miles. About five miles of this distance is covered by carries; the longest carry on this route is about one mile; the shortest, a few rods. If you hire a guide he will furnish a boat and carry it himself. His boat will weigh from sixty to one hundred pounds and will carry two heavy men with all the dunnage you need. He will "take care" of you, as they express it here, and will work faithfully to forward your desires, whether you be artist, tourist, angler or hunter. His charges are $2.50 per day and found [board]. The tired, overworked man of business who gets away from the hot, dusty city for a few days or weeks cannot do better than come to this land of lake, river and mountain and hire a guide.

What the mule or mustang is to the plainsman, the boat or canoe is to guide, hunter or tourist who proposes a sojourn in the Adirondacks. And this is why I propose to mention at some length this matter of canoeing and boating. Being a light weight and a good canoeman, having the summer before me, designing to haunt the nameless lakes and streams not down on the maps, and not caring to hire a guide, it stands to reason that my canoe should be of the lightest, and she is. Perhaps she is the lightest cedar-built canoe in the United States, or anywhere else.

Her stems and keel are oak, her ribs red elm, her gunwale spruce, and six pairs of strips, three-sixteenths of an inch thick, with copper fastenings from stem to stem, leave her weight, when sandpapered ready for the paint, fifteen pounds, nine and one-half ounces. The paint adds about two pounds. She is ten feet long, twenty-six inch beam, with eight inches rise at center; and, propelled by a light double paddle, with a one-fool power in the middle, gets over the water like a scared loon. I propose to take her a rather extended trip before snow flies, if she does not drown me. I reckon her carrying capacity, in ordinary weather, at 150 pounds. If she proves reasonably safe on the larger lakes of the wilderness, she is an achievement in the boat-building line.

She was built by J. H. Rushton of Canton, N. Y., and is by several pounds the lightest canoe ever made by him. I will only add that she is too light and frail. I would recommend ten and a half feet in length, with thirty inch beam, and ribs two inches apart instead of three. Such a canoe would be staunch and safe for one and need not weigh more than twenty-two pounds. She can easily be carried on the head in an inverted position, first placing a blanket or old coat on the head by way of cushion.

When I reached here just one week ago, tired with a twelve-mile ride on the corner of a trunk, while I hugged that frail boat like a faithful lover, I only meant to stop until I could get my traps carried through to the Fulton Chain, which, in the case of the canoe, was not so easy. I was in no hurry—the hotel here [see plate X] is neat, well kept and prices very reasonable. While waiting for the man to turn up who wanted to carry the little craft on his head to the Forge House, it dawned on me that I was well enough where I was for a few days. Parties were constantly coming and going, and all stop at Moose River, which is the halfway house between Boonville and the lakes.

For interviewing guides and taking notes of the region to the eastward, there could be no better point than this; and I needed practice with the canoe before taking her over the larger lakes. Moreover, I came here for a superior quality of water, air and angling, with a little hunting thrown in at the proper season.

What if these things were at my hand, right here, and parties hurrying through post haste to the Brown Tract or the Raquette waters were running away from what they sought? Those coming out of the woods do not, as a rule, claim notable success with the trout. Many of them would eat salt pork oftener than broiled trout were it not for the guides; and one of the latter told me that "trouting" was poor on and around Big Moose, while he thought Little Moose and Panther lakes not worth a visit. "I could catch all the trout I wanted right around here," he added.

So I overhauled my fishing gear and went in for brook trout and, as I supposed, found all I wanted; found that I could, by angling just enough for recreation, catch more speckled trout by far than I need, while there is very pretty fly-fishing at the spring holes in the river. Many gentlemen who go far into the wilderness, at much expense of guides, etc., would be well content with just such fishing as I am enjoying at Moose River. Then there are, within an easy walk of the hotel, several small lakes where deer "water" nightly, and may be "floated" for with a fair prospect of success.

But this is not camping out—not a genuine woods life. We seek the forest for adventure and a free, open-air hunter's life, for a time at least. Well, it may be a little tame, but it is very pleasant and healthful, all the same. As for camping for the benefit of open air, bright fires and beds of browse, fresh picked from hemlock and balsam, we have that right here.

Just under my eyes as I write, there is an island in the river some twelve rods long by six wide. It is well timbered with spruce, balsam, hemlock, cedar, pine, birch and maple. It is one of the pleasant spots that nature makes and man neglects. The island lies high, with roaring, rushing rapids on the left and a broad rock dam on the right, which at low water becomes a cool, clean promenade one hundred feet long by forty feet broad. Near the center of this rock is a natural depression, forming a basin into which the water slowly filters from the river. In this little dock I let the canoe rest at night; against the largest spruce on the island my light tent of oiled factory is erected, and there I rest o' nights—for a few days only, and then for broader waters and deeper woods; perhaps to go further and fare worse.

Forest and Stream, Aug. 19, 1880

Four miles from Moose River on the "Brown Tract Road" there is a trail turning to the right, and a white shingle is marked "Jones' Camp." Follow the trail two miles, and it forks. The left fork is again marked "Jones' Camp." The right fork has a plain shingle, marked with blue pencil as follows: "Wm. Bero, Chief St. Regis Indians." This trail leads to the "Injun Camp," as it is called here. I had met Chief William at the Moose River House; had been told that he could give me more genuine knowledge of the wilderness than any man within fifty miles. I laid myself out to cultivate Chief William, invited him to my room, showed him rifle, hatchet, fishing duffle, hooks, spears, lines and knives. When I showed him an ivory-handled Spanish knife that was really fine, though of little use to me, I saw his black eye gleam; he fell in love with that knife on sight.

I am well used to the American Aborigine. When William had done admiring that knife I made him a

present of it. That won him. I am sorry to say that I
supplemented the gift with a glass of firewater. A cordial invitation to visit the Indian camp followed, with
an offer to carry my canoe and all the traps I desired to
take.

William Bero, Chief of the St. Regis Tribe, heads a
gang of twenty young braves whose tomahawk is the axe
of the backwoodman, whose scalping knife is the spud
of the barkpeeler. Luckily, in going in, I met William
on the trail, who, with a companion, was going in to the
tannery on business.

He went no further. He had promised that if I came
out to his camp he would "take care of me" and he did it.

Relegating his business to his partner, he took my
blanketroll and rifle away from me. He even insisted on
carrying my nine-ounce rod. From the moment I met
him on the trail he took possession of me, so to speak,
and I followed his lead implicitly.

What a grand woodsman the fellow is!

I wanted to go to the Indian camp the first thing. Not
a bit of it. He knew of a spring hole that he wanted me
to fish, and I surrendered. He led me by trails and across
swamps until I lost all notion of compass points, and at
last brought me out on the banks of the Moose at the
mouth of a cold trout stream; and then he explained that
trout had been taken there the present season weighing
over three pounds. I dare say he was right. But as they
had been taken, of course they were not there.

I whipped the water in my best style for half an hour
without a rise, while Chief William, with tamarack pole,
coarse cotton line and large bass hook baited with a
chunk of shiner, stood on a log below me and hauled out

trout after trout in the most business-like and unartistic manner.

At last an unfortunate took my center fly—a queen—and, as I was towing him around, another victim immolated himself on the tail fly—a Romeyn. It was well. With what trout Chief Bill had snaked out we had enough, but it is hard to make any man here believe that you come to the woods for any other purpose than to catch the ultimate trout and shoot the last possible deer. I succeeded in drawing Bill off and we started for the Indian camp. He said it was "a mile 'n half." I think it was. It took an hour and a half of rapid marching to reach it. The camp was simply two bark-roofed log shanties standing among and underneath large spruce and hemlock trees. One of the whirlwinds so common in these woods would make a bad tangle of that camp.

The inmates of the shanties consisted of the fifteen choppers and peelers, with Bill's family of seven—Mrs. Bill, a portly, comely squaw; the daughter, a pretty-featured, plump young squaw with a voice like a silver bell; and four young Indians, the smallest being the inevitable papoose, on his ornately carved and painted board.

That papoose is and always has been to me a Sybilline mystery. I first made his acquaintance many years ago among the Nessmuks of Massachusetts. He was on his board, swathed, strapped and swaddled from chin to toes, immovable save that his head and neck were left free to wiggle. I next saw him among the Senecas of New York State. Then in Michigan, in Wisconsin, on the upper waters of the Mississippi; and now I meet him again in the North Woods. The same mysterious, inscrutable eyes, the same placid, patient, silent baby, varying in nothing save the board, which in Wisconsin was simply a piece of bark. In this case the board is a neat bit of handicraft. When Bill assures me that the carving was "done with a jackknife" I can hardly believe him. And when he says that the bright vermilion, blue and yellow have not been retouched in thirty-five years, I don't believe him at all. The painting is as bright as though it was put on the present season. Commend me to the papoose board. We judge men, actions and things by ultimate results.

After a royal supper of trout, cooked in a manner worthy of Delmonico's, I watched Bill's young bark-peelers as they got red around a rousing fire which they had the good sense to build under a huge hemlock. There was not a pair of round shoulders or a protruding shoulder-blade in the camp. Straight, strong, stalwart fellows, one and all. And every man of them spent the first year of his life on a papoose board.

It has been said a thousand times that Indians will not work, or only in a fitful, desultory way that amounts to nothing; and this is true of the plains Indian; also of the Cree and Chippewa, with other nomadic tribes; but not of the St. Regis or Mohawk and only in part of the Senecas and Oneidas.

As an instance of what Indian muscle can do, let me state that the day before I reached the St. Regis camp ten of Bill's barkpeelers felled and peeled 138 large hemlocks, yielding over thirty cords of bark. In most white camps a cord of bark per day is accounted fair work.

I think the papoose is glad when darkness settles down on the forest and they let up on him. He throws his arms and legs about for all the world like a white baby and crows like mad; then of a sudden his head lops over; he is asleep. I, too, turn in, but not to sleep. Three of the young Indians, including the sweet-voiced maiden, gather around the fire and sing in a low minor key and with soft pleasant voices, the Indian songs of their tribe. And at last I drop into slumber and waken five minutes later, as it seems to me. But it is daylight, and Mrs. Bill has the breakfast nearly ready. I have slept the sleep of the just man and am fresh for the day.

The maiden has got that inscrutable papoose out and is strapping him to his board for the day. When they get him fixed they will pull out from under the roots of a huge hemlock the inevitable jug of tar oil and anoint every visible part of his tawny pelt. The tar oil, well applied, will last some two hours, when it begins to fail, and venomous insects begin to wire in on you.

That papoose understands it. So long as the tar oil lasts he spends his time peering with deep, curious eyes into the gloomy depths of the forest, or, when the wind rises, watching the swaying tree tops. But at the first decided mosquito or punkie bite he gives tongue to a straight, steady yell, without any ups or downs; and Mrs. Bill comes to his relief, takes him between her knees, anoints him from neck to crown, takes him by the basket handle of his board, as one might a peck of potatoes, and stands him up against a hemlock, a log, or the shady side of the shanty. He resumes his eternal occupation of gazing at the mysteries of the forest and is placidly content.

An Indian baby is not expensive in the way of playthings.

Chief William gives me no rest. It is his undying conviction that I came to the woods for the sole purpose of shooting deer and catching trout, and I have got to do it. He hurries me off to Nelson Lake, one of the unmapped waters of the wilderness. There are three spring holes there, in which trout of two pounds have been taken the present season. It is also a good lake for "floating," as they call it here. A short time since a party went on the lake to float and succeeded, by noisy paddling, in scaring six deer out of the lake in one evening, but got no shot. I find Nelson Lake a pretty sheet of water, fringed with the fragrant pond lily that is almost universal here. Bill lays me up to the first spring hole without noise or wake, and I cast my flies across the clear cold water in vain. Chubs and shiners rush madly on the hooks, but trout will not rise. Bill takes a shapeless piece of chub, puts it on that hook of his, and presently drags out a pound trout. To say I am disgusted is putting it mildly. I am swearing mad. He explains that there is a time late in July and early in August when trout "lay deep" and will not rise to the fly. "If we had wums," says Bill, "we catch 'em." That is just my idea, and it happens that I have the "wums." Brought them with me, knowing they were not to be had in the forest. While he is paddling to the next spring hole I take off my leader and replace it with a large hook and strong snell, bait it heavily, and make a cast as the boat glides slowly within reach. It is taken on the first cast, and I bring a half-pound fish into the boat with small ceremony. Bill catches, as usual, a larger one, and then I stubbornly refuse to make another cast. He does not understand it at all, but paddles to the landing and I walk up to camp, scrape acquaintance with his daughter, who is educated, intelligent, and a school teacher among the St. Regis, speaking and writing English fluently. She showed me specimens of chirography and was pleased when I praised her handwriting, which was really fine.

Then I took the papoose by his basket handle and carried him off into the woods. I stood him up against a spruce and made him a speech in mixed Chippewa, Portuguese and English. I explained to him the brutal manner in which his ancestors had roasted and scalped my forefathers and foremothers. I brandished a big knife above his baby head, sang a snatch of Chippewa war song and gave a war whoop. A white baby would have gone into convulsions. He looked at me calmly with those dark, fathomless eyes and when I gave a final whoop, broke into a placid smile that covered his face all over like a burst of sunlight.

An Indian baby doesn't scare much.

After a dinner of trout—again—Bill left me in peace while he went to look after a bark job somewhere among the hills, and I took my blanket, hunted out a dry, cosy nook, rolled myself up and was having a grand snooze, when I was awakened by someone calling my name. It was Ye Chief Bill, and I knew he meant business. He is bound that I shall have sport if it kills me. We are to fish that spring hole again, which I don't care for, and then watch a deer lick, which I do care for. He straps on that everlasting packbasket, gets out his shooting gear, and leads off again, but by a shorter route, to the same spot I fished the night before.

I am sorry to see that Bill's shooting iron is a veritable old musket of the Continental pattern, from which two of the three bands have been abstracted to lighten the piece. He excuses himself for carrying such a clumsy concern by saying that it is the best barrel to throw buckshot that he can find, and he likes a buckshot gun for floating or lick-watching. When I see him load it with about forty grains of powder and eleven small buckshot, I lose faith in him, rather.

At the spring hole it was the same old story. The chief caught two fine trout; I landed one. I refused to throw another fly and began to pack up, to Bill's disgust and surprise. I explain that we have plenty of fish for the trout supper which he has planned, and by the time that is over it will be time to climb up to the blind for lick-watching. He acquiesces, silently stuffs his own traps and mine into that pack-basket and glides up the trail at a pace that keeps my short legs at a half-trot. As we pass up the trail Bill points out a bark-roofed camp on the side hill, where we are to put in for the night. I suggest that it may not be easy to find our way in the dark. "Got lantern," he says, and we glide on. Fifteen minutes of sharp walking and we turn to the right, cross a low ridge and come out on one of the lovely, fairylike spots that one may find every day in these woods. It is simply a moss-covered level bank on the margin of a trout stream, about twenty rods long and half as wide. But what a beautiful dry carpet it was, and the timber, all spruce and hemlock, just far enough apart for shade and elegance, with no underbrush or tangle.

All this was lost on the Indian, who only said curtly: "You make fire. I go over by lick; get some grub there." He disappears, and I proceed to make a fire, selecting a tall spruce with two projecting roots that answer as fire dogs. I soon have the tea water on, and before it comes to a boil Chief William is back. He has a lantern and ample supplies. Diving into the depths of that ever-to-be-remembered basket he brings out bread, pork, tea, sugar, butter, salt, pepper, tin drinking cups, and lastly a large round shortcake.

Shall I ever forget that supper? I still hold the opinion that the trout of this region are the sweetest and best flavored I have ever caught. Also, they are mostly of the dark orange colored sort that I like as regards the flesh. They may be no better than the white fleshed; naturalists pronounce them all the same. But I vastly prefer the rich red color. Supper over, tinware, pack-basket and camp duffle were hurried under an immense slab of bark, and the Chief led off for the lick with the silent, elastic tread of a panther.

NESSMUK

P. S.—I have said little about the venomous flies that render the North Woods a terror and a torment to tourists, sportsmen and naturalists during the summer months. This is probably the country to which Mr. Tennyson refers when he sings of a land "Where each man walks with his head in a cloud of poisonous flies." They are nothing to me. I walk among them through these grand forest aisles safely as in a nunnery. This paper is too long already. If it finds favor I will in my next give a simple recipe by which anyone can flank punkies, mosquitoes and even the black fly.

Foot of Stillwater, Jones' Camp. (Have lost the date.)

Forest and Stream, Sept. 2, 1880

When Chief William led up to the lick he took me by purling streams and pleasant places. Our way led through a beaver meadow—and that same beaver meadow business is an institution, so to speak, found nowhere so frequently or in such perfection as in the Northern Wilderness. On all the waters of the Moose, wherever you find a small stream emptying into river or lake, you may with something like certainty find a beaver meadow on the course of the brook, usually about midway of the stream.

The beaver is the first wild animal of importance to disappear before the white man; but there are men now living who remember when these beaver meadows were beaver ponds, with busy, sagacious, shy inhabitants. At present they are perfectly level meadows, invariably dotted with graceful light green tamaracks, with an occasional spruce, standing singly or in groups of three or four, resting in calm quiet in the bright sunlight, scarcely moved by the furious gales that sweep the mountain tops bare of timber.

From the very apex of Bald Mountain (the Mt. St. Louis of Colvin) you look down into one of these oases, a thousand feet below [see plate XI]. You could almost throw a stone there. Quiet and motionless it lies, while the signal staff on the summit is bending before the gale, and you are fain to keep a few paces from the edge of the precipice lest a sudden gust knock you off your balance and send you into the tree tops five hundred feet below. Far more lovely and interesting to me are these beautiful, lonely nooks than the mountains that overlook them; to me they seem to have been strangely overlooked by tourists and writers who frequent this region. This is digression.

Silently as ghosts we stole through the meadows and

up to an unusually thick clump of spruce and tamarack. Through the thick foliage I looked aloft and dimly saw three rude poles lashed to the branches twenty-five feet from the ground. Silently I commenced to climb, and soon found a seat on one pole, feet trying to rest on another. The Chief sighted a hole through the branches, made his old coat into a ball, and pitched it at my head with a force and accuracy that nearly knocked me off the perch. There was a scrambling among the branches, and the butt of William's preposterous musket appeared in reach. I drew it up, placed it against the left hand spruce with his old coat, and then came the butt of my rifle, followed by the head of the Chief.

We sat silently and watched warily. I saw by his eye that he expected the deer on his side of the "blind" and repented me that I had not placed his coat and blunder-buss against the other spruce. We had not long to wait. The sun was still shining with yellow, slanting rays on the light green of the tamaracks, when, glancing behind and beyond the Chief, I saw the old, old sight—a timid doe in the red coat, gliding cautiously into the tall grass of the meadow, ears forward and nose on the alert for any suspicious taint of enemies. We had been cautious and silent. She detected nothing wrong and turned toward the blind; halted at forty yards between two clumps of tamaracks and stood still to listen and sniff the air.

Now it strikes me that if I were a noble red man and had taken a fancy to a pale face; if I had taken that pale face to my lick for a shot and knew his rifle to be a nail-driver, I would have leaned backward a little and let the white man send a ball into the deer's vitals instead of chancing a musket with eleven small buckshot at a range of forty yards. The Chief did not see it in that light. With a slow, steady motion he cocked and raised the old piece, held it for an instant as in a vice, and then there was a dull, fluffy roar, a great expansion of powder smoke, and the deer was gone. I cared little. She no doubt had one or two fawns waiting for her on the hill; and being burdened with the cares of maternity would be but tough eating at the best. Even had the deer been a buck and in condition I would not have given him twenty-five cents for his shot. He laid the musket with his coat, climbed down in silence, and I saw him for a quarter of an hour hunting diligently for some sign of a hit; but he found not a trace, and he came back looking a little beaten, I thought. Then he spoke for the first time since entering the meadow.

"Watch any more?" he asked.

"No, decidedly no. The smoke settled down on the meadow and the grass is trampled at the very spot where the deer came in."

I pitched his coat and musket into the soft moss, followed them with my rifle, and we started for camp.

"Poor camp; only bark," said William.

I thought differently. It had a good roof of bark, with back, end and sides closed in with the same. We in Pennsylvania would reckon it an excellent camp. And what a grand woodsman the Chief was. He would hardly allow me to lift a stick of firewood, but toted old dry trunks of dead trees, bark and branches, picked browse for a fresh bed, and by the time it was fairly dark we were finally organized for sleep. I kept him awake for an hour beyond his usual time, making him give me points concerning the wilderness, of which he is reputed to have as much and as accurate knowledge as any man living. At length he tired of stories and talk, drew his blanket about his head, Indian fashion, and subsided in sleep.

"Wake me up early; look after deer," he said, the last thing before settling into a steady, subdued snore that was not at all aggravating.

I sat up late—smoked, mused, built fires and listened to my old acquaintances, the owls, until, overcome with drowsiness, I too pulled my blanket about my ears and slumbered sweetly, after the manner of those who rest at night in open camps.

It was daylight when I awoke. I roused first the fire and then Chief William. He shook himself together, borrowed my rifle and was off on the trail.

"'Fi don't fin' deer, be back in hour," he said, laconically.

"A fool's errand," said I, and went down to the spring hole to try fly-fishing. I pooled a couple of half-pounders, came back to camp and cooked a trout breakfast in my best manner. William had been gone more than his hour, breakfast was ready and hot, and I was getting impatient when far from beyond the beaver meadow on the mountain came the plain, sharp crack of my rifle. He had found the deer after all. And I ate breakfast alone.

It was past 9 a.m. when, getting impatient, I started up the trail and at the first turn met the Chief, a smile of Christian satisfaction on his face and the limp half of a freshly-killed deer wagging at his hip. It was a bit of good hunter craft. He explained how he had quartered the ground like a setter for a hundred rods before finding blood. Once found, he had followed it like a sleuth-hound, losing it again on the ridge, and finding the deer at last by patiently quartering the ground again. It was badly wounded in one kidney (all luck), but made a short run and lay down again. He crept up within thirty yards and shot it through the head. Few white hunters would ever have tracked out and killed it.

William cooked himself a hearty meal of venison, of which, being well fed, I could not partake; and then, still insisting on carrying my traps, started to put me, by a short cut on the trail, to my next objective point, Jones' Camp.

Albert Jones came into the wilderness about three years ago, so sick and weak as to be lifted from the wagon and unable to speak aloud on his arrival at the Forge House, foot of the Fulton Chain. He had been a strong man with an iron constitution, and, like many Americans, had broken himself down by constant overwork and anxiety. He had been a business man; a miner in the early California days; a ranchman; had owned and run sawmill; had been a tamer of wild horses among the Spaniards and "buckies" of Mexico, and had spent the best part of an active, vigorous life in the multifarious pursuits, chances and changes perculiar to an adventurous American.

It came to an end by a general physical breakdown. The doctors said "general debility." They always say that when they are stumped. Jones was a native of Northern New York and in his younger days had often gone to the wilderness for sport and recreation.

When hand and brain could work no longer he said, "Take me to the woods; if I am to die, let me die there." They took him in to die. In less than two months he had so far improved as to go out and attend to business, which had rather piled up on him in his absence. One month of that settled him. He was down again, and again he "broke his holt" and came to the woods. Again he got the benefit of an open-air, carefree life, and when he thought himself pretty well able to manage his affairs he went out of the woods and got down to business. And it floored him in just three weeks. Then he let go and came to the Wilderness for good, as he says.

He built a comfortable log camp (or house) at the foot of the Moose River stillwater, built and bought half a dozen boats, keeps boarders (when they come) at most reasonable rates, and passes his time as quietly as any man I know of. He has regained health and spirits and would, on the whole, make an excellent subject for "Adirondack" Murray if that gentleman were writing another book.

His place is situated at the foot of navigation for the Fulton Chain, and it is a twelve mile paddle from it to the Forge House landing, foot of First Lake. I will only add that of all the camps I have eaten and slept at, none has so good a supply of goodsized brook trout as Jones' camp. And thither I hired Jones to back [pack] my eighteen pound canoe and knapsack for a trip to the other side, or as much of it as I might find interesting and profitable.

I might mention that I made the acquaintance of a young man at Jones' who is a permanent boarder there, having sought the forest for relief from asthma, from which he had been a great sufferer. The relief was found, and he is another witness to the great benefit so often derived from a residence in the Wilderness.

Not all invalids improve by coming here. I had a pleasant camp of bark, with open front, pointed out to me on Fourth Lake, where a young man affllicted with incipient consumption tried all last summer the effects of open air life in the Wilderness. His camp was pleasant and in a healthful location. There was nothing lacking for a fair trial, and he tried it long and fairly, but in vain. He sleeps with his fathers. Scores come here for health who will tell you frankly that they might as well have stayed at home. Very many receive decided and permanent benefit. Some bad cases of asthma and consumption in its first stages are apparently cured. One thing is certain: you pay your money, you do not always take your choice.

From Jones' I proposed to start on a canoe trip through or into any part of the woods that might strike me as interesting or desirable. In pursuance of which plan I paddled off from Jones' landing one exceedingly fine morning, reaching the Forge House [see plate XII] in time for dinner and realizing pretty fully the difference between up stream or down when the paddle is in question, especially as I got fogged on the course and paddled sixteen miles instead of twelve.

The Forge House, kept by J. W. Barrett, is the starting point for most parties who go to the Fulton lakes. The house is well kept, and it is a great rendezvous for guides, whose boats may nearly always be seen at the landing, where the owners come to pick up their parties.

En passant, as this is the season both for lakers and brook trout and as many are deterred from visiting the woods at the best season for fishing by those intolerable nuisances, flies and mosquitoes, I may as well fulfill a promise made in my last, of an infallible recipe for these pests, by using which one may walk the trails and climb mountains, fish by day and sleep by night, free from the poisonous stings of black fly or mosquito. I know there are a score of remedies all more or less effective, and I have tried most of them during the last twenty-five years. The one I have found most effective is made as follows:—

Three ounces castor oil and two ounces best tar. Bring to a slow boil on the stove in any vessel, letting it simmer for half an hour. When partially cool, add one ounce of pennyroyal, and mix thoroughly. To use, pour a teaspoonful into the palm of your hand, rub your hands together, and then rub every exposed inch of skin with your palms. A light coating will do; and don't wash it off. You may have to repeat it once or twice daily for the first two days, but after that one application each day will leave you in peace. It is in no way filthy, and it is not disagreeable to most persons, while the effect is all that can be desired.

Forest and Stream, Sept. 16, 1880

The camps of the Wilderness deserve a special notice. Their name is legion and they are increasing at a rate that defies calculation.

Let us start at the very foot of the Fulton Chain, not at the Forge House, but below, at the huge dam controlled by the State, and used to draw off the lakes for public use, i. e., to feed canals, reservoirs and other State works, as may seem good to those in power.

Passing through the marshy pond at the foot of First Lake you enter the channel proper, now one and a half miles, and pass Indian Rock, the spot where "Old Foster" shot his Indian after a quarrel at the Arnold Place, four miles below. Rounding the rock you have on your right evidence of the effects of civilization and progress. Stretching away to the dense green timber of what is now the mainland, there is a desolate waste of dead, decaying trees, lifting their bare broken arms toward heaven in ghastly protest against the arborean murderers who tortured them to death by slow drowning.

Motionless in the fiercest storm, they stand with their dead feet and legs in the dull, sedgy marsh. Almost imperishable, they have stood there for more than a generation, and a generation yet unborn will see the same ghastly sight. The sight is such a picture of desolation that, paddling down the lake by moonlight, I am careful to be always looking the other way.

On the Woodhull lakes, on the Beaver, on the Oswegatchie and a dozen other waters, the same desolate sight pains the eye of any tourist or lover of nature who may chance to pass these wearisome "drowned lands." But more of this anon.

The line of dead "hop poles," as they put it here, extends for about a mile, with a trend to the southward as you pass into the clear water of First Lake. Rounding the bend of dead timber, you see before you, across the lake a high pine-clad, sandy point, with a flag flying above the top of a tall thick pine. Below are buildings of some pretension. Two well-appointed log houses, one for the guides, cooking and dining, and the other for the family, men, women and children, to occupy. There is an excellent boat house; another building is a good storeroom and icehouse: the whole affair is well appointed, pleasant, healthful and costly.

When I first visited "Camp Stickney" Dr. Nichol's party were in possession. They were employing three of the most experienced guides at a cost of $45 a week and board. They were not eager anglers or hunters, but took their sport in a reasonable, gentlemanly way, and their icehouse was never without a supply of trout and venison.

Rounding the point on which Camp Stickney stands, you see at your left, halfway up Second Lake, a poplar-covered sandy bluff. Passing this you come in sight of the Eagle's Nest, the most noted landmark on the Fulton Chain. The oldest guides could not tell me how long the nest had been there. For several years the birds deserted it, owing to the fusillade kept up by the cockneys of the Muggins tribe, who usually considered it the correct thing to empty guns and revolvers at the eagle's nest, occasionally hitting a young eaglet. The thing is better ordered now. With one exception, no one has fired at them this summer, and I saw them day after day as I was watching for deer, standing on the edge of the nest, flapping their callow wings and screaming for fish, which the parents brought them in quantities that made one a little curious to know just how many pounds of fish it took daily to supply that aerial camp.

Passing the Eagle's Nest you have, on your right, another of those dreary wastes of drowned lands and dead timber, of which the only good thing you can say is that the dreary spot is a good place to float for deer in summer and affords duck shooting in autumn. Turn to the left, leave the dead trees astern, and Third Lake camp, or "Buell's Camp," is before you, a mile distant. It is an old camp, known in the guide books as the "Grant Clearing." It has stood for many years, has been occupied by more parties than I care to name, and is, to my thinking, as pleasant a site as any on the Fulton Chain.

I made the acquaintance of the present owner, A. G. Buell, at the Forge House. He had come in simply to look after his property and go out again as soon as he could make some business arrangements. He was alone, and lonely. He did not like to cook; thought of going out in a day or two unless he could raise company to stay with him. Now, I like to cook, can do it well, and I wanted a quiet place to lay off, paddle, fish, float and possess my soul in peace. Inference is obvious. I paddled up the Third and became domiciled at Buell's camp. It is one of the pleasant episodes I shall not forget. But this is digressing.

Every boat that passes up or down these lakes must of course go up or down by inlet or outlet, and they must pass directly in front of Buell's camp. Passing up the inlet, it is about eighty rods from this camp to the foot of Fourth Lake, and passing along the northern shore of this lake, rounding a sandy point marked by a solitary dead pine, you come to the Snyder, or Cold Spring camp. This is one of the high-toned camps already mentioned, and to the southward, at the foot of the island opposite, is the "Camp Chapin"; a party consisting of two young men from Rochester, with consumptive tendencies. I stopped there several times and found that their guide, Fred Rivett, was faithful in the performance of his duties so far as the supply of trout and venison was concerned; but I did not detect any coughs or other evidence of pulmonary difficulty. The vitals of the party seemed, to an outsider, all right enough. But I noticed a decided consumption of victuals, with some drink. By the way, it is claimed that the trout, or salmon, are larger and of better flavor in the Fourth than in the other lakes. And I may mention that the Chapin camp guide stands "high hook" on the Fourth, with a salmon weighing twelve pounds as his record.

But a word for the Little Moose Lake. The largest salmon caught in these waters was caught on Little Moose, by a Mr. Miller. The fish weighed, by scale, twenty-five and a half pounds, and was of excellent flavor.

The average of these lakes, which it is sacrilege here to call anything but "salmon," is just about two and a half pounds. And they are exceedingly fine on the table, better than speckled trout to my thinking, in which I am corroborated by nearly every guide and angler on these waters. I have passed by the camps on Little Moose. They are three, with open bark camps that any one may occupy, thrown in. And it is one of the finest lakes on the Moose waters. Passing up the Fourth, the first camp above the Snyder is Sam Dunakin's—Honest Sam Dunakin. Whiskey-loving Sam, one of the oldest guides in the Adirondacks. Faithful to his party, be the same a party of one, or comprising women and children, with the nuisance in the shape of *pater familias* thrown in. Always competent, always sober (on duty), no guide can take you to more places by more direct routes or "take care" of you better than Sam. God forgive him the fearful lies he tried to get down me, as he, being out of a party just then, got me to paddle up and pass the night with him.

The next camp is Ed Arnold's [see plate XIII], across the lake, in a pleasant grove, and with accommodations for a rather large party. Ed is, and has been for many years, a guide, and one of the oldest. Born on these waters, he has passed his life in the Wilderness. Like

Mitchell Sabattis, Sam Dunakin and others of the old guides, the routes of the wilderness to him are as streets of the city to a cockney. He keeps a woods hostelrie, but takes parties to guide, and he guides them well.

The "Lawrence Camp," the "Turin Camp," the "Pratt Camp," the "Bissell Camp," all on the Fourth, are but repetitions of those already described. If these camps give any correct idea of the way and manner of living in the North Woods at the western side, how is it on the other side, where daily lines of stages bring loads of passengers each day; where horses and men are stationed at the "carries" to take guides, boats and parties across; and [where] telegraph wires, steamers, high-priced hotels, billiards, boats, pianos, croquet grounds and all the concomitants of a high-priced watering place prevail?

The days of the hermit hunter have passed away forever so far as this wilderness is concerned. The deer are disappearing rapidly and the trout are being thinned out at a deplorable rate.

It is true that the camps able to employ skillful guides manage to have a fair supply of trout and venison, but it costs them more than a dollar to the pound. All the same, it is a dreamy, sylvan, delightful life to live, and not as expensive as Long Branch or Newport; but, to my thinking, far preferable.

And what of the guides—the men who honestly and earnestly believe themselves entitled to the rights of sovereignty over the whole domain of the Northern Wilderness? And are they so very far wrong? One guide said in my hearing, "We take our parties to the houses that treat us best. They always go where we say. If a landlord wants to go back on the guides, well, he can try it on."

Yes, the guide is a leading and controlling element of the North Woods. He has salient points of character well worth noting because, sooner than he thinks, perhaps, his vocation will have passed away. Already on the eastern side of the wilderness he is out of the regular jobs so easily obtainable in the days of "Murray's Fools," and even now, on the western side where the independent system prevails.

The wilderness guide deserves special note. He is a specimen of the genus homo that I have nowhere else seen; and, whatever he may think, destined soon to pass away forever. His present conviction is that the advent of first-class hotels, stage coaches and steamers is fated to ruin the guide business, and he is doubtless right. At present he remains in pristine vigor, and it is worth while to note his most prominent characteristics while he is to the fore.

Firstly, your guide must be familiar with a portion at least of the leading routes through the wilderness. Secondly, he must have the muscle of a cart-horse, because the third requisite is a boat of the "Long Lake model," weighing, with oars, seats and neck-yoke, eighty-five to one hundred pounds. Argument will not convince him that the world can produce a better or lighter boat fit for guiding. Show him a Rushton model, light, strong, weatherly and weighing forty-five pounds, and he will say she is slow; he wants a boat that he can "get somewhere with." It does not occur to him that he is working for a party who would much prefer a more roomy, safe and comfortable boat, and that if he made somewhat less speed his party would be just as well satisfied, while it would lengthen his job and lighten his "carries"—just what he desires.

And so he fits himself for guiding and awaits his "party." If he be an old and well-known guide, probably he is engaged to meet a party say at the Moose River House or at the Forge House. At the appointed time he is on the spot, his boat cleanly sponged, himself in condition to take care of his party of one or two. Suppose you are the party—of one.

Business detains you and you are a week behind the appointed time. "It is of no consequence—not the slightest." Your faithful guide is there with his boat and has a bill against you as follows: "Guide's services, $18; Hotel, $7." You are a little sore, but conclude to make the best of it; and, after all, is it not just? You made the bargain and appointment. Guide has been faithful to his tryst. You can not get out of it honorably; so you succumb and, being bent on a good time, get cheerful and invite guide to "take something." You are on the right tack there. One of his best "holts" is to take something. But you have had enough of hotels; you did not come for that, and you suggest an immediate start.

Guide is ready—has been ready for a week. And he commences emptying his old shirts and overalls from an immense affair, looking for all the world like an exaggerated fish-creel and holding a full bushel. This is the inevitable pack-basket of the wilderness. Shaped for the human back and holding a bushel of provisions, clothing or anything you choose to put into it, without jamming or mussing it, it is far ahead of any knapsack I ever carried. But beware how you fill it, because when your guide carries an eighty-five pound boat, with a gun and a fishing rod or two, across a heavy carry, the pack-basket will either fall on your shoulders or you will have to "double the carry." You do not understand that as you order bread, butter, canned goods, tea, sugar, coffee and all the eatables you can think of or the festive land-lord can suggest, until the guide hints that the pack-basket is about full. Then you desist and begin to con-trive how to carry your extra clothing, etc. The guide is constant with advice and assistance.

When the basket will hold no more, he makes up your extra duffle in a neat blanket-roll and announces his readiness to start. As you take your share of the dunnage to the landing, it dawns on your mind that you might have got along with less weight; but it is too late to mend that, and you place the impedimenta amidships of the long, cranky boat, creep into the stern while the guide holds the bow firmly, and, guide seizing oars, you are off up the lakes at a speed of six knots an hour.

Your destination is Beaver [River] *via* Raquette and Forked Lakes; thence across by the ponds and carries from Little Forked Lake to Little Tupper; then by Charley Pond to Smith's Lake and the Beaver. Guide advises a different route, taking in Long Lake, Big Brook, Slim Pond, Stony Pond, etc. You go over the map with him and accept the change. It is a longer route, but more pleasant; takes in more country and there is less carrying.

At the head of Fifth Lake you begin to realize what a carry means. Guide hauls his boat out in a way that means business, makes oars and seats fast, dons his neck-yoke, takes as much more as he can possibly handle, and walks off with the inverted boat covering him from sight—all but his legs. Your load is the pack-basket, a blanket roll, gun and rods, weighing seventy-five to eighty pounds, not less. Before you reach the upper landing the perspiration is running from every pore, and you are winded.

A rather long pull over the Sixth and Seventh restores your wind, but when the boat is hauled out for the carry from Seventh to Eighth, which is over a mile, you snivey on your load. You can't stand such infernal loads in hot weather. You will carry the basket over first and come back for the rest. Guide thinks you had better take it all at once; it just makes three times as much trouble to "double carry," and you can go slow and rest as often as you please. And again you follow a pair of legs and a blue boat over a carry, arriving at the Eighth Lake in a limp and exhausted state and with a firm resolve never to carry that load again.

Arriving at the carry from Eighth Lake to Brown's Tract Inlet, you proceed to divide your load accordingly and express your unalterable resolve to double trip the carry anyway. Guide is all sympathy and complaisance. "You needn't do that," he says; "just take your rod and gun. I'll come back for the basket and roll while you rest. You ain't used to packing." Sure enough. Why not? You have engaged him for two weeks at $3 per day and found; you are to pay him for a week you did not have him. What odds can it make to him whether he puts in more or less of the time making carries? Thus you reason, and reason soundly, to my thinking. But the average guide can Daball [Daboll? Probably from Nathan Daboll, author of arithmetics; here used in the sense of "run up"] the sum total of a trip through the woods in a way and manner to strike a professional accountant dumb. Well, you have "come down." Henceforward you are as wax in the hands of your guide.

You sit down by the sluggish water of Brown's Tract Inlet and claw madly at punkies and black flies while guide doubles the carry. After this he doubles all the carries, and you take it easy. It is what you came for. Very pleasant it is to be rowed at leisure through a wooded, romantic, mountainous country by a man who knows the lay of the land, the best places for "floating" and all the favorite springholes where trout do most abound. You are never short of trout, and guide promises you a shot at deer as soon as you get a little off the main route.

He takes the best of care that you get neither wet, tired or hungry. You are his party. For the most part you stop at one of the many forest hotels for the night, where they will cook your trout in the best manner and give you food and rest at which no reasonable man will cavil.

And so through the long, pleasant summer days, just cool enough for comfort, you glide over these tiny summer seas, up inlets, down outlets, down clear streams, not hurrying, ignoring time, losing the date of the month and day of the week, until at length, with little fatigue and much pleasure, you arrive at your destination on the upper waters of the Beaver.

Guide has an interest in a good bark camp here, to which he takes you, and while you try your fly-rod at a springhole which he shows you he proceeds to make the camp comfortable and arrange matters for a ten days' sojourn in camp. Your fishing is a success, and when you return you find a pleasant fire, fresh browse on the bed, and all your multifarious traps arranged just to your notion. Guide cooks a trout supper that you think equal to anything you ever tasted, hastily disposes of the dishes, dives into some recess in the back end of the camp and brings forth a jack with material for a light.

"You must shoot a deer to-night; this camp needs venison," he says. You are agreeable.

"Ever shoot a deer by jack-light?" he asks.

You confess you never did. Then he instructs you how to do it. The gist of which is, be perfectly cool, shoot when he tells you, and by all means *aim low*. Most people overshoot by jack-light, he remarks. Before 10 p.m., at which time you are to push out, you begin to get a little nervous, but at last guide announces that time is up, and the oars are laid aside. Light burning brightly at the bow, you are placed properly with final instructions, and the boat glides silently into the clear water of the lake.

For ten minutes you move thus, and then the low lisping of the lily pads, as they are slowly sucked under by prow or paddle, becomes just audible. Fifteen minutes of this—twenty, perhaps—and the guide whispers hoarsely, "There's a doe; see her?" The boat is swinging slowly to the right, and—yes, there she stands up to her belly in the pads, her eyes looking like illuminated blue glass. "Shoot," says a hoarse whisper behind you, and you shoot. There is a plashing and spattering of water, a trampling on the bank, and the doe has vanished. For once the guide loses patience.

"Why, what ails you? The deer wasn't four rods off," he says, crossly.

"Damfino," you answer, in the same spirit. Guide recovers his temper at once.

"Never mind; we'll find another," he says.

You are not so sure. But the boat, impelled by that noiseless paddle, glides over weeds, grass and pads for nearly an hour, and there, right before you, stands another deer. This time you are wiser and cooler; guide says nothing. He sees that *you* see, and the deft manner in which he quickly and silently turns the boat, that you may shoot without changing position, is a perfect piece of woodcraft.

Again there is an explosion of saltpeter and brimstone, followed this time by a continuous plashing and floundering in the water that bespeaks a fallen deer.

"You've got him this time; nice yearling buck," says the guide, cheerily.

Yes, you have got him. Half a dozen large buckshot through shoulders and "lights" have finished his running.

Guide soon has him in the boat, and you start for camp, the direction of which is a sybilline mystery to you; but ten minutes of vigorous paddling brings you there, and guide says, "Now you turn in; it's after midnight, and I ain't going to get you tired out and sick. Turn in; I'll take care of the venison." You obey, believing you are not at all sleepy, however. But in five minutes you are asleep, and the sun is shining brightly when you next open your eyes.

Guide is missing. Going to the spring you find him there, and he shows with some pride his cellar, where he has neatly stored the venison. It is a *cache* in the side of the ravine, scooped out with much pains and labor, and cool as an ice-house. "It will keep meat fresh more than a week," he says. And he is right. And just here it dawns on your mind that your vacation is gone. You came to the North Woods to recuperate, to botanize, to climb mountains and live for a few days a free, careless life of the Daniel Boone type. Well, you have caught and eaten trout to your satisfaction, and you wanted a change to venison. You have it. What humane excuse can you have for catching another trout or floating another deer until your present supply runs short? Even if you desired to do it your guide would go back on and discourage every attempt at fishing or hunting. He will tell you plainly that deer and trout are getting too scarce to be wasted.

And so, with a week's time ahead of you and the knowledge in your heart of hearts that hunting and fishing were the main incentives that brought you here, you refrain from both. Notwithstanding, the time passes pleasantly—you row and paddle, climb the hills, go over to the next lake, smoke, sleep and eat—ye gods, how you do eat—and rest, and enjoy yourself. You half wish the venison would spoil, that you might have an excuse to shoot another. But guide takes care of that. And what a cook the fellow is.

"It's lucky we brought the potatoes and onions," he says. "They were a little heavy on the carries, but we couldn't make a stew without them."

And his soups and stews are about perfect, while his broiled steak is a thing to "thank God on." Just at the last end comes in another party of two, with a guide, and your guide, seeing that you have more venison than you can use, divides with them liberally, and after a long visit they go over to the next lake, where they are to camp.

On the following morning you pack up and are off to Wardwell's, where you discharge and pay off your guide and go back to civilization again. You are in no hurry; guide's time is not out until sundown, and you take it easy. But when you come to settle in the evening, you find relations have slightly changed. Hitherto you had been guide's special charge and care. Now his time is out; he must look for another party. You call for his bill, which he makes out as follows:—

"You know," he says, "there was a week I waited at the Forge House. Call that $18 (it was really $21); paid my own expenses, $7, makes $25. Fourteen days guiding, $42, makes $67. Then there was extra work; guess I'll call that $10—ought to be more."

"Extra work?" you ask, in blank astonishment.

"Yes," he says, calmly. "Doubling the carries. You see yourself that every time you double a carry it makes just three times the distance to go over. For instance: Brown's Tract Inlet, mile and a half. Go back an' *come* back again, three miles, making four miles and a half; an' jess so with all the carries I made from there to the Beaver. No gentlemen, ever since I was a guide, ever asked me to do that work without being willing to pay for it."

You are beaten; remonstrance is useless, and you succumb.

"What else?" you ask.

"Nothin'," he says; "only my return pay, three days. That's understood, of course. Three days, $9, and expenses—dollar a day (that's reg'lar)—makes $12. Sixty-seven, ten's seventy-seven, an' twelve's eighty-nine. That's the bill—eighty-nine dollars."

There is no use in quarreling or remonstrating. While you were his *party* he took care of you as a father would care for an invalid son. When his time ran out and you were off his hands, you became at once his *placer,* his greenback mine, to be panned out and worked down to the ultimate dollar. You pay $12 return money. He gets away at once, rows up to your late camp, lays in a day's supply of bread and venison, makes himself comfortable for the night, and the next morning at sunrise he starts for his return, for which you have paid him $12.

Now, how does he make it? I can tell you. He shoulders his boat and makes the carry to Twitchell Lake, seven miles; crosses that, and makes the carry to Big Moose Lake; down Big Moose, and by carry, and the North Branch lakes to Fourth Lake of the Fulton Chain; down the lakes, Fourth, Third, Second and First; and by 9 p.m. he is at the Forge House, where he started with you two weeks before. He has taken $12 of your money for return and expenses, and he has made it in one day, without expending a cent save what he may pay for whiskey before he goes to bed. As for yourself, you sit down and count the cost about as follows:—

Expenses from Boonville to Forge House........$	7.50
Bill at Forge House.........................	1.00
Expenses from home to Forge House...........	8.00
Hotel and supply bills, *en route*................	27.00
Pay of guide...............................	89.00
Expenses from Wardwell's place, with hotel bill..	7.50
Expenses home	8.00
Whiskey, cigars, flunkeys and omnibus..........	3.00
	$151.00

You have killed one deer and caught many trout. You have had two weeks of delightful recreation. Trout and venison have cost you more than they would at Delmonico's; but they were fresher and eaten with a far better appetite. As for the delicious air, the free, open-air life, the lakes, the scenery, the balsam-laden breezes, the sweet sleep at night, these can not be estimated by money. "You pays your money and you takes your choice." I will only add that the above sketch is not a fancy one. It is all, substantially, fact, made out by actual daily estimate of the gentleman whose trip to the woods it outlines, and gives a rather favorable view of a successful tour for two weeks through the Northern Wilderness.

The gentleman went home a week since, and the guide passed the camp where I write, three days ago, rather proud of his achievement in making the Forge House from Beaver River in one day. Let me quote from the melancholy Jacques in "As You Like It": "A fool, a fool! As I do live by food, I met a fool i' the forest. Oh, noble fool, motley's the only wear."

Forest and Stream, Nov. 18, 1880

Yes. Let us leave the hot pavements, the baking, blistering walls and sweltering sleeping, or sleepless, rooms. Let us, i' God's name, take to the cool waters and calm shades of the forest.

> For brick and mortar breed filth and crime,
> And a pulse of evil that throbs and beats;
> And men are withered before their prime
> By the curse paved in with the lanes and streets.

And lungs are smothered, and shoulders bowed,
In the poisonous reek of mill and mine,
And death stalks in on the struggling crowd,
But he shuns the shadow of fir and pine.

["October" from *Forest Runes*]

It was on the morning of the last seventh of August when I started from Third Lake to fish for salmon, as lake trout are invariably called here. The weather could not have been fairer. I was well organized to fish a buoy of my own, with an informal permit to fish others, and I had not the slightest intention of doing anything else. And just here comes in the fascination of this happy-go-lucky, care-free sort of forest life. You never know, or care, one day what you are going to do the next.

After a delightful paddle through First and Second Lakes, I passed the Eagle's Nest and entered the Third. Then it occurred to me that I had a blanket-roll at Sam Dunakin's camp, consisting of gum coat, blanket, pocket hatchet and revolver. It was a good time to get the traps. Fourth Lake is at times rough. Now it was smooth. Sam is one of the oldest guides in the wilderness, and of course we had a chatty sort of visit, which made me a little late in paddling out for the Third Lake.

Now, a short mile below Dunakin's camp is the cold-spring, or Snyder camp, which I had a standing invitation to visit. As I was passing, Mr. M., the head man of the camp, hailed me with a cordial invitation to land. I did. Found the cold-spring camp rather a high-toned affair for a forest residence. There was an ice-house, a good boat-house and a log-house that would be a palace to an early settler. They had a guide who, like most guides, was an excellent cook; and of course I was not to be let off until after dinner. I wish to record the fact that the best lake trout I have eaten in the wilderness was at that camp. They were also capable of a glass of good wine, and people of culture, withal. What wonder if it was 4 p.m. when I said good-bye and paddled out into the Fourth?

Then it struck me that I had a seven mile start toward Blue Mountain Lake, with such weather as I might not get again for a month. True, I had no supplies, but they could be had at Arnold's, some two miles above, and I struck across and up the lake for Arnold's place. Got some lunch, arranged my duffle for a trip, and paddled out for a log camp I knew of at the foot of Fifth Lake. It was getting dusk when I struck the Inlet, and by the time I reached the camp it was nearly dark; but I found the camp in good condition. There was fresh browse and plenty of dry birch wood, with a roof invulnerable to rain.

I had no tea or coffee, or any sort of dish; but I foraged an old tomato can and made a pot of hemlock tea, had a glorious fire, and a night just such as a woodsman loves. There was not a soul within miles of me, and the shriek of the steam whistle was afar off, beyond the keenest ear-shot. The owls were plentier than usual, and in exceptionally good voice, while a loon, just above in the Fifth, kept up his strange wild cries at intervals through the night.

At daylight I repeated the dose of hemlock tea, finished the little lunch I had left, and paddled up the Fifth Lake, which is only a frog pond of some ten acres.

From Fifth to Sixth Lake there is a carry of three-quarters of a mile, which rather turned my hair, for it was a warm morning. But from Sixth to Seventh it is clear paddling. From Seventh to Eighth is a stiff carry of one mile and twenty rods, according to the best informed guides, and before I got over this I was pretty well winded.

At the landing on the Eighth I met a young man, one of a party of two engaged on the Adirondack Survey, who very considerately invited me to his camp for dinner. It was well. Like Falstaff when he took a foot command, I was "heinously unprovided," and I felt too weak and tired to make the tedious carry from Eighth Lake to Brown's Tract Inlet without food and rest.

I found the two young men encamped in a shanty tent on the south side of a point which makes out from the mainland, and their landing so hidden that they were not likely to be bored with visitors. Stayed with them two hours and got partially rested; also was feasted on pork and beans, and paddled around the point to the carry, not feeling very well competent to make it. To a strong, well man it might have been a trifle. To me it was most exhausting. I arrived at the landing on the Inlet so tired and beaten that I lay down on the leaves for more than an hour before launching out. I found the Inlet to be modeled after the letter S, with an occasional oxbow thrown in for variety, and a dull, sluggish stream, deep and dark, fringed with aquatic plants, shrubs and dank cold grass, with not a place in its course of four miles where I would like to venture a landing.

At last the broad Raquette lay before me, dotted with green islands, and with its quaint bays, points, headlands and islands so mixed and mingled to the eye that although my directions had been lucid I was puzzled just which way to steer. My destination was Ed Bennett's, and I was to turn a green island which lay to the left, when I was assured I would see his landing with a flagstaff and flag, which on the larger lakes is the usual sign of a forest hostelrie.

I saw no flag, but afar off what looked to be a new building and from thence came a sound as of one who drives nails into resonant boards. As I live, it turned out to be a new church in the course of erection on an island. Just where the congregation is to come from I can not say, but preachers are plenty enough here in the summer, and perhaps it is well that they should have a regular house of worship somewhere in the woods in order to keep their hands in while doing the wilderness.

At length, after much desultory paddling, I sighted Bennett's flag and made my best time for the landing. It was time; the wind was rising, and Raquette Lake can get too rough for a ten foot canoe very easily. I was surprised to find Bennett's as well furnished and more neatly kept than many a first-class hotel in larger towns on the direct line of railroad travel. Table, beds and rooms were furnished forth in a manner that left little to be desired, and when it is remembered that all supplies must be brought by a long and expensive route from the eastern side of the wilderness, his terms seem very reasonable. Two dollars per day, or ten to twelve dollars per week, are Ed's figures, and having been a guide for years he knows just what the tourist requires better than a greenhorn.

But alas! For the romance of paddling through the forest alone in an eighteen-pound canoe.

Before I was half rested my ears were pained, my soul

was sick with the shriek of a steam whistle, and a small steamer rounded to and made a landing after the manner of small steamers outside the Adirondacks.

The little canoe serves as a letter of introduction all through the woods, and I soon struck up an acquaintance with the pilot of the steamer—she wasn't large enough to sport a captain—who said, "You don't want to paddle that cockle-shell over this lake. Put her on deck and come with us." And I did. I was very tired and far from strong. It seemed silly to do so much hard work needlessly, and I went the rounds of the little steamer with the unpronounceable name [probably the *Killoquah,* built by William West Durant in 1879 for runs on Raquette Lake and the Marion River]. Across the lake we made another landing — Kenwell's — and found another hotel, new, neat, well found and moderate in price. Kenwell's terms are $1.50 per day, $7 to $8 per week, and his place is very pleasantly located. From Kenwell's to the Forked Lake House landing, and here I struck tourists and guides in force. Leavitt was full to overflowing. I could find a place to sleep after some managing, and the table was excellent; but people were becoming too numerous, and I had a suspicion that I had left the wilder part of the wilderness behind me when I left the Eighth Lake.

Game and fish were by no means plenty. The Forked Lake House had a corps of guides employed, but they could not keep the house in fish or venison. I did not take either after leaving the Fulton Chain. All the same, every tourist had his breech-loading battery, and a full supply of rods, reels and lines, which is a great comfort to the average tourist and does small damage to trout or deer.

From Forked Lake I went by steamer mostly to the

carry on the Marion [River], made the carry, and found another little steamer [see plate XIV] to make connections on the up-river side. Went on board of her and became resigned to steam and a teeming civilization that increased nearly every hour.

Passed up the Marion through Utowana and Eagle Lakes and saw an old settled farm and an ordinary farm house on the northern shore of the latter, which being the only imitation of a farm on the trip usually induces inquiry. You will be told that long before the grand rush of tourists and the advent of costly hotels this place was cleared and occupied by "Ned Buntline." Here he secluded himself during a part at least of every year for many seasons; here he did his literary work, and the place is, and probably always will be, known as the "Ned Buntline Farm."

A very clear and beautiful sheet of water is Blue Mountain Lake. It has often been called the gem of the wilderness. But its days of natural wildness are gone forever. There are three large hotels on its banks filled to overflowing with guests. Lines of stages leave daily for different points to the eastward. All luxuries of the season are to be found at the hotels, and billiards, croquet, boating, lounging through the groves, singing and piano-playing give the shores of the lake quite a Long Branchy air. Besides the hotels there are private boarding-houses, while many families have private residences on the prettiest sites on the lake, which they are pleased to call camps.

The Blue Mountain Lake House, kept by a genial, thorough landlord, once a guide, had a hundred and fifty guests, and, more coming in, the house was overcrowded. John Holland is not the man to turn anybody out of doors, and he worked hard until nearly midnight to stow the whole party away for a comfortable sleep. Chairs, sofas, lounges, and finally the dining room floor were utilized, and at last the ultimate citizen was quieted. I succeeded in getting a short lounge with a back-breaking bend in nearly the middle of it, but could not get so much as a cotton sheet in the way of bedding.

I went down to the canoe, got my tent cloth and gum coat, wet with the heavy dew, put the dry sides next me and turned in; soon got warm and slept soundly.

Of the other hotels, the American, just across the bay, had up eleven wall tents, all of which were full, and the house overrun with guests. The Blue Mountain House (Merwin's) was also full, as well as every boarding house; and some of the guides at 11 p.m. took their blankets and went out to seek a spot to camp in for the night. And little more than eight years ago there stood a bark shanty just above, the only sign of human habitation on Blue Mountain Lake. Speaking of this rush to the Northern Wilderness in '79, Colvin says, "Where one came last year, ten come this, a hundred the next." He is just well right. You meet them everywhere. They permeate every accessible lake and stream, and it is hard to say what lakes and streams are not accessible. You meet them in the most out of the way places, just where you expected to be alone, and always the breech-loader and fly-rod which they hang to like grim death.

Said an old guide to me, "If they averaged one deer to three guns there wouldn't be a deer left in the wilderness at the end of three years." Said another guide, one of the oldest and best, "What few deer are killed here had better be killed by parties who employ us; it encourages them to come again." And P. Jones, guide to the Stickney camp and one of the most intelligent, spoke thus: "We don't care to kill many deer ourselves, or to catch many trout. Just enough for use. When we hunt for market we go to Michigan, on the Au Sable. Killed twenty-five there last fall, and am going again when the guiding season is over. The deer in these woods are worth more to us guides alive than dead. They are worth fifty dollars a head as they run." That is about the view taken of fishing and hunting by the average guide in the North Woods.

As I had come to do the lake and the mountain, I concluded to go through. Climbed Blue Mountain on a hot August morning and on arriving at the verge found Colvin's lookout ladder, made by nailing cross strips to the trunks of two spruce trees. It was rather an old affair and looked shaky, but I went up and took in the view, which was really extensive and fine; and then I followed the trail which leads to the signal on the highest point of the mountain, climbed the signal and tried to make out the twenty-eight lakes I had been told I should see, but could only make out about half of them. As to mountain peaks, the number was rather confusing than satisfying. They ran together and over and by each other in a manner to throw an ordinary mind into a state of temporary imbecility.

I could dimly discern Marcy, and I thought I identified Mounts Haystack and Skylight. But they rose in such innumerable and unknowable billows, peaks, points and ridges, that the mind—at least my mind—can retain only a confused recollection of them. It had been hot work making the ascent. It was cold and windy on the summit of the mountain, and the immediate surroundings were cheerless and desolate. One entire summit had been slashed in 1873 to give an outlook for the signals of the survey, and the dead, decaying trees, lying just as they fell, were not pleasant to look upon.

There was an excellent bark shanty between the spruce ladder and the signal, and in a swampy depression near the summit under the edge of a boulder, I found a pool of cold spring water which rendered the bottle of water I had brought from the hotel quite superfluous.

I had done the mountain, and it seemed the proper thing to do the lake. I did it. I paddled in and around among the islands, landed up and launched out again, greatly to the delight of the youngsters, who were there in force with parents or chaperones and who were exceedingly taken with the little boat; and then I ignobly placed her on the deck of the round-sterned little packet and paddled by steam to Ed Bennett's landing on the Raquette. And then it came down to the double blade again.

After a night's rest and an excellent breakfast I started out to cross the lake, and rather got down on my muscle, for the wind was ahead and rising. By the time I got into smooth water at the mouth of Brown's Tract Inlet it was getting rough, and I was glad to be in the tortuous but safe inlet once more. A tedious paddle of four miles, a weary carry of one and a half, brought me to the Eighth Lake. Wind ahead and hard traveling. Another tiresome carry of a mile and over and I was on the Seventh, with the wind strong and the second largest lake of the chain to cross. I was a long time making it, and was almost too tired to make the next carry from Sixth to Fifth, but I finally shouldered the canoe and made the distance slowly and wearily to the Fifth, which at least ended carrying for that day. It was well that the wind went down with the sun or I could not have made the rough and stormy Fourth, which often drives the best guide boats to land. As it was, the canoe pitched and danced about quite lively, and it was nearly dark when I landed at Ed Arnold's, on the south shore of the Fourth.

The Fourth, by the way, is the largest lake of the chain and is famed for its lake trout. Arnold's is a central point for catching them, and he is an experienced guide. His terms are low, one dollar per day, or even less by the week. He has buoys at the best points near the house, at which you can fish as much as you please, and you are supposed to bring your fish to the house. A night's rest at Arnold's, a pleasant canoe ride down the Fourth, through the placid Third, by the Eagle's Nest into the Second, by the Stickney camp into the First, with its dead timber and long marshy outlet, and at 9 a.m. I hauled in at the Forge House landing, well pleased with my Blue Mountain trip, but with no idea of repeating it this season. I can do better.

Forest and Stream, Nov. 25, 1880

It is the 2nd of September as, sitting in my shanty at the foot of Fourth Lake, I lazily scribble a few notes of a two months' paddle in these Northern waters. I have perhaps paddled too much. My unquenchable love for fresh water seas — large or small — has kept me from prospecting the forest as much as in all honesty I ought to have done.

But the *Wooddrake* [*Nessmuk No. 1*] was such a duck; it was so delightful to drift about the cool, clear lakes by day or night in her. The weather during the heated term was so perfect, and the woods from side to side, and from end to end, are so fearfully heavy to a footman that I came to spend most of my waking hours afloat. More times than I can tell I filled her with the coarse, soft brakes (ferns, botanically), piling them a little more at each end of the canoe than in the middle, then lying down in the easiest position I could get, and let myself drift—just where it pleased winds and waves to send me.

The easy, gentle rocking of the canoe was the best incentive to drowsiness I ever found, and by night or day was nearly certain to send me into dreamland. A score of times I have gone to sleep drifting on deep, wide water, to be awakened by the pressing and bumping of the little craft among the dead balsams and spruces that—Sathanas confound them—make half the shorelines of all the lakes in the North Woods a nuisance instead of a delight. Government does it. Authority decrees that because a certain ditch on which boats may be floated, taxed, locked, loaded and, let us hope, ultimately sent to the demnition bow-wows—requires more water, the most beautiful and useful water system in the world shall be laid under contribution for the needful liquid to float a bull-head scow. The bright green shores are to be converted into a dismal nightmare of "drowned lands." The outlet of First Lake has a most powerful and commanding dam which has lowered the first three lakes forty-one inches since July 12th. A dam is being built at the foot of Sixth, where there is a sixty foot fall or thereabouts.

A coffer dam is in progress between Seventh and Eighth, the Woodhulls, the Beaver, the Grass, the Oswegatchie.

All the waters in the western and northern portions of the wilderness are "essentially damned." As to the short-sighted policy that has caused this, time will show. For the present I am tempted to quote from "As You Like It": "Touchstone—'If thou be'st not damned, for this the devil will have no shepherds. I cannot see how else thou should'st escape.'"

I cannot dwell on this dreary feature that every intelligent tourist sees and execrates. If Verplanck Colvin's proposition of a grand aqueduct from the headwaters of the Hudson to New York City (supplying the Hudson Valley) should ever become an accomplished fact, it will change the entire character and status of the Wilderness in a manner that guides and landlords have yet to learn.

Never in the history of the Wilderness was such an influx of visitors seen as in the summer of 1880. One naturally asks, is this to continue? When "Murray's Fools" rushed to the North Woods in 1869, it was thought by many, even the guides, that the thing was overdone.

In 1870 guiding was poor business. It has picked up wonderfully since then, but to my friends, the guides of the North Woods, I want to give a few words of advice. I have made it a point to get my information from the men most able to give it, and these are the guides. My good fellows, don't run yourselves into the ground. You know, and I know, that when the guiding season is over, instead of $3 per day you are ready to "hire out" for the winter at a wage of $1 per day and board, and few of you can get that much.

More: when you skin a gentleman, he pays the swindle and makes a note of it.

For weeks I fished, paddled and hunted about the

headwaters of the Moose. My soul was sated with trout and venison. I longed not for the fleshpots of Egypt, but for the vegetable gardens at home, green peas, so to speak; succotash, as it were; the early harvest apple; the sweet bough; the summer sweeting; the fresh tomato; the dozens of things unattainable in the woods. All this I said to myself as at midnight I sat at the outlet of Fourth Lake and hailed and interviewed guides and tourists who row over these waters at all times of day and night.

It was the fourth of September. In a week more my holiday was out. Why should I stay longer? I had camped on the outlet of Fourth Lake until there was nothing new there. The immense timber cut by Government to dam the lakes had furnished me chips and bark, within six rods of my shanty tent. Intelligent, cultured men had stopped at my camp daily to see the eighteen-pound canoe and the little pennymite who had paddled her over five hundred miles without a guide. I wanted one week on the Stillwater of the Moose River. Why, it was just the time to start. I built a fire that marked my last chance at Government chips and could be seen for miles, put my duffle in shape and at daylight struck out for Jones' Camp, eighteen miles below.

I stopped at "Buell's Camp" on the Third to bid the quiet old owner a last good-bye, and I had a last argument with Perrie on the relative merits of our favorite flies. But, having quarreled with him all over the Fulton Chain (because he held me in the rain while he fished his deuced spring holes and I was in his boat and couldn't get away), I will do him the justice to say that he can furnish the best cast of flies for the Moose River waters that I know of; and he can throw them at the end of sixty feet of line in a way that puts me quite in the background. I have no interest in the fly business, but I like a good cast for the particular waters I am fishing on.

From my camp on Fourth Lake to foot of Fulton Chain, seven miles, one hundred rods carry, and twelve miles to Jones' Camp—a little over nineteen miles. But *facilis decensus averno* [the descent to hell is easy]. Not that Jones' camp is *averno* at all; but the descent from the Forge House is delightful and *facilis*. Coming down I stopped at the old deserted house marked on Colton's map as the "Arnold House." For years this was the headquarters of guides, hunters, trappers, surveyors, tourists and speculators. How many of the present generation who pass by the doors of this old building have the least idea of the tragical events connected with the old house and the large, sandy, weed-grown clearing about it?

The buck-boards that almost brush its sides as they pass it stop there no longer. The Forge House, two and a half miles above, is the present starting point for the Fulton Chain and the Moose waters. But there is not a house in the State with such a record as the old "Arnold place" [see plate XV]. Here it was that Joseph Harisoph [Charles F. Herreshoff], after losing a princely fortune in the vain attempt to make a fortune out of the plentiful iron ore hereabout, shot himself in despair. And here it was that "Old Foster," after his quarrel with the "Injun," "skinned out for the Point," as the guides put it.

"The Point" is on First Lake, nearly two miles from the outlet, and it is four miles from the Arnold place to the outlet by water, with a carry of eighty rods, while by trail it is two and a half miles. The quarrel had been bitter. Knives were drawn and blood shed, but hunters and guides were there in force and the men were kept apart.

"You never see Christmas," said the Indian, fiercely.

"You never see to-morrow," said Foster, as he took his rifle and disappeared in the forest.

When the Indian left the Arnold place with his canoe, two friendly whites went with him. They did not really suspect danger; but, as they were passing Indian Point, single file, three canoes, the Indian in the middle, Old Foster rose up with rifle at his shoulder. The Indian gave a yell, dropped his paddle, and only said, "Me dead man." Even as he said it Foster's bullet whistled through his lungs, and he tumbled into the water dead.

Every man who goes up the Fulton Lakes knows "Indian Point" and "Indian Rock." I have passed them more than a score of times this summer and never without a thought of the tragedy that occurred at this spot. Because it happened that Foster, after a tedious tournament in the courts on a trial for murder, got clear on a plea of self-defense and came to Tioga County, Pennsylvania, to finish his days, being justly afraid of the Indians who had sworn his death.

Lastly, there is the room where the elder Arnold, father of "Ed" and "Ote" Arnold, "Brown's Tract guides" of the present, shot and killed the guide, Short, in a foolish quarrel about a dog chain. It was a brutal deed, and no man here has one word of excuse or extenuation for it. The family say that after the shooting Arnold went into the bush, directing a daughter to hang a white cloth out of an upper window if his victim died before sundown. Short died about 3 p.m., the cloth was duly hung out and Arnold went over to Nick's Lake, weighted himself heavily with stones, and waded out of his depth, coolly drowning himself. There was a coffin buried at Boonville, anyhow, and a funeral attended by the Arnold family as mourners. But the prevailing opinion is, here, that the funeral was a sham and that Arnold, who knew the woods to perfection, calmly walked over to Canada, that being quite as easy and more agreeable than to drown himself.

Quite a tragical spot is the "Old Arnold Place." I spent a couple of hours wandering about the sterile clearing, counting and inspecting the rooms, noting the broken furniture and discarded tin or iron ware and the moldy boxes, barrels, etc., that remain as they were left in the large and commodious cellar. The ruins of a dozen castles on the Rhine would have less interest for me.

There was a rusty scythe hanging in what was once the drawing room, and in an upper room was a bunk, well filled with soft dry grass. An old tin pail, half full of ashes, had recently been used for making a smudge, and the bunk had been used within two or three days by some sleeper who had come to the clearing to watch for the deer which feed at early morning or late evening in the lonely fields.

Below the house is the landing—not on the main river, but on a small pond with an outlet to the Moose, easily rowed or paddled—and this landing is almost classic. For a time beyond even the oldest Indian tradition, this has been a favorite landing for the red men; but the birch is seen here no more, and even the narrow blue boat of the guide goes up the channel but seldom.

Halfway from the Forge House to Jones' is "Little Rapids," and twenty-five rods above the rapids there is, on the left bank, a clear, dry, spruce-covered point. Just here there is a good runway, and as I swung around in sight of the point there he stood! a plump little yearling buck, already beginning to show the *short blue*, and within forty yards of me. He let me drift down within five rods of him and then, raising his flag, whistling and snorting his loudest, went off with a succession of high, defiant bounds. My rifle was back at the Forge House and the revolver, which would have done for him, was tucked away in my knapsack. Ah, well! Let him live. I have had my share of venison, bear meat and trout even if I never taste either again. Only one does not like to miss such a chance.

By the time he was out of hearing the rapids claimed my attention, and, shooting swiftly down the narrow channel, I glided into the deep, smooth water below for as pleasant a six-mile paddle as one could wish. The weather was perfect, the banks thickly studded with trees, mainly spruce and balsam, and I caught frequent glimpses of beaver meadows, with the light, graceful foliage of the tamaracks showing beautifully as a background to the dark, sombre evergreens of the river banks. The six miles was passed too quickly, and I ran the canoe into the tiny landing that Eri Jones had prepared for her, let him take her to the boat house, and laid away the paddle, feeling that my canoeing was over for the season. I have not stepped into her since.

Jones' camp is pretty nearly a forest solitude. A high

hill to the south, across the river; another to the north and east, and deep, heavy woods on all sides. It is emphatically a place of rest. The low, constant murmur of the rapids, a hundred yards below, is audible at all hours of the day and night. To me it is somnolent music. Often, when Jones and his son were off fishing, I dropped asleep over pen and paper, lulled by the low, unvarying monotone of rushing waters, and at night it was better than an opiate.

Here I rested, fished a little, wrote less, and loafed away my last week in the woods. It is worthy of mention that we had brook trout on the table every day of my stay. I got to care very little for them. In common with the majority who come here, I much prefer the lake salmon. We made the evenings shorter by exchanging notes. I have been something of a wanderer by sea and land, while Jones is a Forty-Niner, has been a tamer and catcher of wild horses, and was in the thickest of the fight at the Panama riots, when Walker's actions got two steamerloads of passengers into the hottest kind of water and cost nearly or quite a thousand lives.

He is well posted, too, on the North Woods and matters pertaining thereto, and he gave me some interesting and instructive points not laid down in the books. Owning a camp, with boats to let and being on the guide list himself, he could give stories and incidents concerning the guiding business quite amusing and perhaps slightly suggestive to the prospective tourist. For instance, take the following, for the truth of which I can vouch.

Dick Cragoe [Crego, in plate XVI] is a Brown's Tract guide and a good one. Last season he had a party consisting of a gentleman and his wife who came to the woods for rest, recreation and amusement, and as usual the gentleman brought a breech-loader, with which he was anxious to kill a deer. But his vacation neared a close and he had been unable to get a shot. The lady, who was his constant companion in boating and fishing excursions, also desired to see how it was done, for once, and thus the gentleman said to his guide:—

"Dick, I can't go out without shooting a deer. Get me a shot to-morrow and I'll give you five dollars."

Dick got the dogs out early, while he lay off on the lake with his boat and party to cut the deer off. The hunt was a pretty fair success all around—even for the deer. The dogs succeeded in driving the deer (a doe, as usual) to water. Dick succeeded by rapid rowing in cutting her off and getting a "tail-holt," which, by the way, is a favorite "holt" with the average guide, and the gentleman emptied his six-shot repeater at her head as Dick held on to the tail—and actually missed with every shot.

Then the woman was aroused. "Cragoe," said she, "it's a shame. Let her go and I'll give you more than my husband gave for his shots."

Dick knew his little biz, and he knew her word was good as gold. He loosened his grip on the tail and the doe scuttled through the lily pads, climbed the bank and was soon safe in her forest home. The gentleman paid his five dollars like a man, and next day the party went out. On leaving, the lady handed Dick a package, saying, "Don't open it until we are away." The package cotained a fine silk handkerchief with the name of Dick's wife neatly worked in one corner and also a ten dollar greenback.

Dick's account of the hunt borders on the humorous.

Plate I.
Nessmuk's home in Wellsboro, Pa. Razed in the 1930's.

Plate II.
Nessmuk paraphernalia on exhibit in the Bailey Hotel,
Wellsboro, Pa., 1942.

Plate III.
Nessmuk's monument in the Wellsboro, Pa., Cemetery.

Plate IV.
J. Henry Rushton.

Plate V.
The Rushton Boat Shop, Canton, N.Y.

Plate VI.
Canoes under construction in Rushton's boat shop.

FEATHER-WEIGHT CANOES.

NESSMUK.

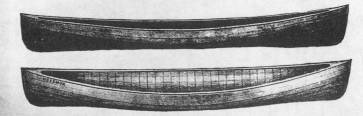

DIMENSIONS—Length, 10½ feet; beam, 27 inches; depth at ends, 15 inches; depth amidships, 9 inches; weight, about 18 to 22 pounds.

MATERIAL—Keel and stems, oak; planking, white cedar, 3-16 inch thick; gunwales and inwales, spruce; decks, white cedar; ribs, red elm.

CONSTRUCTION—Lapstreak; ribs very light and spaced 3 inches; very short decks; no inside floor.

FITTINGS—1 ash folding seat; 1 double-blade paddle, fitted with drip cups.

PRICE—$27.50.

Plate VII.
A page from the 1903 Rushton catalog.

Plate VIII.
The *Sairy Gamp* on exhibit at the Adirondack Museum.

Plate IX.
The *Wee Lassie*.

Plate X.
The Moose River Hotel.

Plate XI.
Third and Fourth Lakes of the Fulton Chain of Lakes
from the top of Bald Mountain.

Plate XII.
The Forge House.

Plate XIII.
Ed Arnold.

Plate XIV.
Steamboat at outlet of Blue Mountain Lake.

Plate XV.
Ruins of the Herreshoff Manor.

Plate XVI.

Ned Ball

Merle White

Jerome Wood

Peter Rivett

George Goodsell

Jim Dalton

Frank Smith

Wellington Renwell

Phil Christy

Bill Dart

Dave Charbonneau

Dick Crego

Plate XVII.
Mitchell Sabattis.

Plate XVIII.
A group of guides at Blue Mountain Lake.
Mitchell Sabattis stands between the trees.

Plate XIX.
Alvah Dunning and his cabin on the island in Eighth Lake.

Plate XX.
Grove House, Long Lake. David Helms carries the guideboat.

Plate XXI.
Corey's "Rustic Lodge" in 1885.

Plate XXII.
Bartlett's Landing, the "Sportsmen's Home."

Plate XXIII.
Paul Smith, 1878.

"It was," he says, "one of the most satisfactory hunts I was ever into. The man got six shots at a deer, fifteen feet off, at less than a dollar a shot. Anybody would give that much. The lady was satisfied and well pleased, while the doe ought to be. It stood me in nigh on to twenty dollars, and I don't feel as I ought to be dissatisfied if the deer did get away from us."

Dick would feel insulted if anybody should hint at cheekiness or extortion.

Another case of deer hunting came within my own knowledge in August last. "Slim Jim," a muscular guide of the Forge House clan, had a party of one, a Mr. George B....., of Philadelphia, who was rather profitable, Jim's bill footing up to about $65. Jim was faithful, took good care of his man, and did not overcharge him. Therefore, when Mr. B.... expressed an earnest desire to shoot one deer before going out, it was Jim's bounden duty to get him the chance. As floating was a failure they went over to the North Branch Lakes, with Jim's old speckled hound for a right bower, to try driving, and there met another party with Si Helmer for guide.

Helmer's party had killed deer before and were anxious for venison rather than the fun of shooting it. Therefore, when Jim explained that his man was very desirous of shooting a deer and asked Si to assist, it was agreed that Mr. B.....should have a shot if possible. It turned out quite possible. The doe—a doe again—came to water a long way from the boats and made for the opposite shore. By dint of his best rowing Helmer succeeded in cutting her off at the last instant and turning her out into the lake, where he got the tailhold and waited for Mr. B..... to shoot. One would suppose that the merest tyro who ever fired a gun might be able to shoot a deer in the head while it was held fast by the tail, but the shooting of the tourist is often fearfully and wonderfully done. Mr. B..... put a heavy charge into the doe's hind quarters within a foot of Si Helmer's hand; pretty well destroying a hind quarter of venison and drawing some very energetic remarks from Si.

Slim Jim was stopping at Buell's camp, and on the return of the party Mr. B..... remarked, with a satisfied air, "Well, you can score one for me." I should say so. Small wonder that the guides have, as a rule, little faith in the shooting of their parties, at least until they have been tested by actual trial.

If these rough notes find favor, I will at another time give some hints for parties who wish to go, in light boats or canoes, through the wilderness without guides.

Forest and Stream, Dec. 8, 1881

CRUISE OF THE NIPPER

She met me by appointment at Boonville. With praiseworthy punctuality—considering her sex—she had arrived several hours before me. The express agent assured me that her conduct had been most exemplary.

The tourists, male and female, were just then thronging into the Wilderness from either side. Everything on the Northern road brought its quota of seekers for pleasure, recreation or health. The *Nipper* was interviewed remorselessly. Well dressed ladies, neat young girls, and even children approached her irreverently. They examined her graceful lines. They made comments on her unknown owner, and invariably ended with lifting her gently by the nose, with exclamations quite irrelevant. No gentleman tourist passed her by without critical examination and comments. As they raised her carefully, they said—if they were worldlings—"Holy Moses! who's going to paddle *that* eggshell?" Clergymen said: "I do declare! Is that intended to go on the lakes?" The ladies remarked, "Oh, my!" "Did you ever?" "Dear me!" "What a beauty!" etc.

None noticed the little gray-haired fellow who, dressed in coarse blue flannels, smoking a clay pipe, dangling his short legs off the platform, and reading the last number of *Forest and Stream* was quietly taking in the thing— until the agent pointed him out as the Skipper of the light craft they were admiring. He was immediately interviewed, and questions were frequent and fast.

"Do you expect to live in her on Raquette Lake?"

"Can you stand rough water?"

"Can you throw a line from her, and handle a good sized fish?"

"Isn't she too frail?"

"And what is that little green canoe in the corner? She looks still smaller."

The Skipper answered the last question first. The little green canoe is the *Nessmuk* that was paddled last summer over 550 miles, came out tight and staunch, was taken 230 miles to northern Pennsylvania by rail, paddled on the rocky affluents of the upper Susquehanna, and is going back to the Wilderness, still tight and seaworthy. The second question. Yes, she is frail. She is in-

tended, both by her owner and builder, to be the lightest
canoe of her dimensions ever built of oak, elm and cedar,
with light spruce gunwale. (Here the Skipper showed a
letter from her maker, Rushton, expressing doubts as
to her strength, and giving pen and ink diagrams of the
way she might be strengthened by bracing, thwarts, etc.)

"But," said the Skipper, growing enthusiastic, "she
don't need strengthening. The two pairs of strips nearest
the keel are of full thickness—three-sixteenths of an inch.
The third pair taper a little toward the gunwale, and the
three upper pairs run light, very light. Her weight is sixteen pounds; length, ten feet, six inches; beam, twenty-
eight inches; rise at center, eight inches; at stem, thirteen
inches; ribs, forty-five inches. Gentlemen, if any of you
are canoeists, you know that you have no business to put
weight on the upper strips or the gunwale. All weight in
a light canoe must come on the keelson, and the first
two, possibly three, pairs of strips. The *Nipper* is strong
enough for me. As to throwing a line from her, she is the
very best possible craft for fly fishing. You can make a
ten-ounce trout tow you in any direction you please until
he floats helpless. I have done it in the *Nessmuk*.

"As to rough waters and squalls, I expect to stay as
long as the average guide boat of the Adirondacks and
ride more steadily in a short, sharp sea."

With expressions of sympathy and hopes that they
might see the light canoe and her Skipper on the lakes,
the tourists went off on the inevitable buckboards, and
the Skipper began to organize for a cruise. It was necessary to make the first twelve miles of it overland, and the
route was not pleasant. Hills, hollows, sand up to the
hub, boulders, and six miles of corduroy road. Such was

the first twelve miles—as every man knows who has made the route from Boonville to Moose River.

The trip was made in and on a lumber wagon, with the canoes packed in straw and guyed with heavy twine, the Skipper kneeling on the port side and keeping a death-grip on the gunwale of the *Nipper,* unmindful of the hemlock lee-board that was steadily abrading his spinal column. The charge for the tow was four dollars, with a stipulation that the horses should walk all the way. When the latter clause of the contract was enforced by the Skipper, the disgusted driver relieved his feelings by a twelve-mile string of oaths that would have struck a Missouri Bullwhacker with paralysis.

It is a weary trip, that road from Boonville to the "Tannery." But it has an end; and both driver and canoeist felt better when the two canoes made a landing on Tom Nightingale's porch without crack or scratch. A double nip of whiskey quieted the driver, while the hearty greeting of Jolly Tom, Si Holliday, Charley Phelps, Colonel Claskin, and a dozen others made the Skipper feel as though he had got home.

Moose River is not by any means a bad place to stop at. The hotel is well kept, family very pleasant, and charges reasonable, let alone that pretty fair trout fishing may be had in several spring brooks easily reached in an hour's walk. It took four days to work these brooks and a few spring-holes in the river, the result being a reasonable supply of fine brook trout, saving none under six inches.

The road from the "Tannery" to the foot of the Fulton Chain is so rough that no prudent tourist will send a light canoe in by the buckboards, and boats are usually sent in from the west side, via Jones' camp, on the shoulders of guides. And even in this way they do not always get through safe. There was a fine new boat sent in that way last July in which the guide contrived to knock an ugly hole. So the Skipper decided to send his duffle by buck-board to the Forge House, make the nine-mile carry through the woods to Jones', and paddle the twelve-mile stillwater to the lakes, which he did.

In fact, he overdid it by taking the right-hand trail when within three miles of Jones' and carrying the *Nipper* over to Little Gull Lake. This lengthened the carry to twelve miles, but the visit to this lonely, beautiful lake almost compensated for the extra labor. It was late in the afternoon when Jones' camp was finally reached and the Skipper learned that the camp was bare of trout. Pork, potatoes and tea were indulged in to a moderate extent, and the night's rest which followed was of the soundest.

The next day was spent in a faithful but vain attempt to inveigle a mess of speckled trout from their old haunts in the Moose; and it was remembered with regret that these same haunts gave a daily supply of trout on the previous season. Everywhere, so far, trout had been found less plenty than in the summer of '80.

A second night of sound sleep at Jones' camp, and the *Nipper* was put afloat for the first time, her owner boarding her rather cautiously for a canoeist who has faith in himself and his craft. She proved marvelously steady, however, and a paddle up-stream of three and a half miles in one hour brought her to the carry around the flood-raft and gave the Skipper confidence in her steadiness. The Forge House landing was easily made inside of four hours, and, once in the boat-house at Barrett's, the cruise of the Fulton Chain was fairly commenced.

And here let us drop the third person singular and pick up the Eternal Ego, that I am as sadly weary of as my readers possibly can be.

At the Forge I met very many whom I knew last season; also, many who were visiting Brown's Tract for the first time. Among the latter were invalids of the Lung Disorder type, who did not seem very favorably affected by the damp, chilly weather which prevailed during July and well into August of the past summer. As to the brigade of consumptives who came to the Northern Wilderness last summer in search of health, which they were destined not to find, I shall have something to say further on. Many were induced to come through reading a magazine article entitled "Camp Lou," and the disappointment felt by most of them was sad and bitter. [The article, by Marc Cook, was published in *Harper's* for May, 1881. It is an invalid's story of a seemingly miraculous cure, and it excited so much interest that it later was expanded to book form under the title of *The Wilderness Cure*, New York, 1881.]

It was 4 p.m. on the 16th of July when I paddled out from the Forge House for a rather extended cruise through the Fulton Chain, Raquette Lake, Forked and Long Lakes, the Raquette River, Tupper Lakes, and, by a circuitous route, back to the Fulton Chain. It was a very pretty program, destined to be carried out only in part.

The afternoon was gusty and stormy. Black, wind-laden clouds went whirling across the sky with ominous speed, and I heard a guide remark, "Uncle Nessmuk ain't anxious to take this in." So I made my gum coat

into a cushion and struck out. For a mile and a half up
the channel the canoe flew along smoothly with the wind
dead aft. Then came the open water of First Lake, white
and spumy, with short, sharp seas, that I must take fairly
abeam to the inlet, where I could see the waves dashing
white over the large boulder at its mouth. I hesitated for
a minute about trying for the inlet. But it was the trial
trip of the *Nipper*. If she would swamp in a blow, better
do it on one of the smaller lakes, and I pulled out. When
fairly out of the roughest water her behavior surprised
and delighted me exceedingly. She rose and settled on an
even keel with a steadiness I should have scarcely looked
for in a boat of twice her size and threw off the steep,
sharp seas like a duck. I thought then, and still think,
that for a light, comfortable cruising canoe, under paddle, her model cannot be improved.

When about half way across the lake a low, ugly looking black cloud came up from the southwest, and when
just over the lake let go a torrent of water that drenched
me to the skin in three minutes. It was no time nor place
for struggling into a gum coat, and I wanted both hands
on the paddle, so I took it as philosophically as possible.
It ceased as I rounded the rock at the inlet, and I went
flying up Second Lake with the wind astern, only dipping
the paddle for steerage way; and again there came a
thunder gust with a down-pour of rain. But, as I could
be no wetter, I rather enjoyed it.

Rounding the Eagle's Nest, I ran under the lee of the
forest-crowned point and sponged out the canoe, for she
was getting logy with the water that had fallen into her,
and then paddled across to Third Lake camp. Perrie,
with several old acquaintances, met me at the landing

and gave me a woodland welcome, besides lending me dry clothes that I greatly needed.

I found the camp enlarged to thrice its former capacity and filled to overflowing with boarders and tourists. Four of the inmates were suffering with pulmonary troubles and did not seem to be getting much benefit from "balsamic breezes" or "ozone." Each one had his or her peculiar cough; the season had been wet and cold, and the bright, open-air fire that should be inseparable from a camp in the wilderness was, for the most part, lacking.

On the night of my arrival the wind shifted to northeast with a cold drizzling rain, and in less than forty-eight hours after landing I had joined the little band of coughers, coughing oftener and louder than any of them. As I had made the trip to the woods for health mainly, this was most provoking. I thought it was only a surface cough, so to speak, but it was constant, hard and irritating. There were plenty of cough remedies in the house, and I tried them all, with little or no effect until I resorted to balsam, taken directly from the little blisters on the balsam fir, soaked into sugar and allowed to percolate slowly down the throat. This gave relief, and I mention it for the benefit of any future tourists who may get landed upon a cruise by a cough and cold.

By the 22nd I was sufficiently recovered to assist at a dinner given at Dunakin's camp, on Fourth Lake, by Messrs. F. J. Nott, S. F. Fish, and M. M. Crowell. The dinner was entrusted to Sam Dunakin as cook and purveyor, and it was a neat affair. The guests, estimated at six, turned out thirteen strong at the table, State Game Constable Dodge being one of the number, and I thought he looked a little glum as he tasted the "mutton," which had a rather gamy flavor, as though it "had lain in the roses, and fed on the lilies of life" (or of the lakes). Whatever he thought, he said nothing, and the dinner was one of the pleasant episodes one never forgets. Our hosts were capable of good red wine, with a bottle of Martel at the finish. The trout were excellent and well cooked, and all three of our hosts sang glees in capital voice and good taste, aided by the game constable, who, by the way, struck me as being the right man in the right place. Just at dark I paddled leisurely down to Third Lake with the impression that the 22nd of July, 1881, would be a good day to mark with a white stone.

Next day I tried salmon trout at the buoys and brook trout at all the spring holes, with no success. In fact, the fishing on Third Lake after the first of July was not worth the trouble of putting a rod together or wetting a buoy-line.

Forest and Stream, Dec. 15, 1881

The *Nipper* was up for a rather extended cruise, to start July 3. I quote a brief entry from my journal under date of July 23: "Slept later than usual and on rising found my knapsack missing. The loss is irreparable. Spent the day paddling around the lakes trying to trace it. It has gone to Blue Mountain in the duffle of Mr. Durant and his guide Moody—taken by mistake." The guides assured me it would come back by the first boat coming from Blue Mountain, or, perhaps, the Raquette. The mistake was a most natural one. The knapsack was of oiled ducking, black, not heavy, and easily taken as a part of the oilcloth goods that hung on the same large nail. I was fain to wait with what patience I could.

Days passed, and the knapsack did not come back. I put the time in by climbing the hills—Bald Mountain especially; paddling, botanizing, digging blisters off the fir trees for the few drops of balsam contained in them, and fishing for lake and brook trout—with little success. I interviewed guides and tourists, studied maps of the Wilderness, and strove—in vain—to keep dry. To give an idea of just what the weather was like at this time, I will give a few brief quotations from a journal kept faithfully on the spot:

July 16th. Gale with heavy rain. Frequent showers; wind mainly from the north.

17th. Heavy wind and cold rain from the north, everyone shivering with cold. Five people in the house with hard, chronic coughs. Bark, bark, all night.

18th. Rain, rain; blow, blow, from the north, as usual. Cough, cough. Five of us keep it up. Two will most likely never be better.

19th. Like the 18th, cold and rainy. Rained all night.

20th. Put on a gum coat, took my little hatchet, and went for the woods. Made a fire that would roast an ox, and got nearly dry—for once. Still raining. Rains nearly all the time. 'Tisn't the most favorable weather for lung diseases; not the healthiest region, I should say. Parties who come for health are every day going out, disgusted and sick. Still the camp is full.

21st. John D. Fraser visited us. He has been taking views of the scenery in Brown's Tract, and taking them well. But what American pays for American sketches? Let him go to Switzerland or the Rhine. He painted, artistically, a name on my canoe; for I hurried her maker so that he did not have time to do it, and I would as soon have a wife or daughter without a name as an unnamed canoe. Still it rains and still we *miserables* cough night and day. Is it cheery? Do we feel exhilarated? "Like the Grank Turk?" as Mr. Quilp remarks. Not to any great extent, I should say.

22nd. Weather a little better. Better myself. Dinner at Sam Dunakins's. Warmer. Wind S.W., and showers during the night.

23rd. Already noted.

24th. Paddled to Forge House. Wet again. Am wet all the time. The whole Wilderness water-soaked.

25th. Just a repetition of 24th for rain and wind. Tried the spring holes just before and after sundown—with the usual luck. Guides, boats and parties coming and going all the time.

26th. More parties and more rain. Many going out disgusted. Tried fly-fishing again—with no luck.

27th. Weather better. Am making up a blanket-roll and getting ready for a good start to-morrow, if it is fair.

28th. Rained in the fore part of the day, but cleared off in the afternoon and I started for a cruise at 6 p.m.— rather late, as I found; for, what with stopping at Ed Arnold's for a visit and loitering on the way, night overtook me long before I reached the head of Fourth Lake. Here I found a roaring torrent coming down the inlet from Fifth Lake, which after an hour of hard work, I was unable to stem, and so drifted back into Fourth Lake, where I paddled around until midnight, finally landing on an island where Fred Hess has a good house and camp. Here he lives with his family; but happening to be absent just then, could not welcome me, so I made myself welcome to his open camp, found a lamp and a good bed, lighted the one and took possession of the other, managing to put in a few hours of solid sleep before sunrise.

Started early and tried the inlet by daylight; but the current was too stiff, and I was forced to back down and take the carry to Fifth Lake. Found the fishing camp at the foot of the lake partially submerged and untenable. Last year it was a fine camp to stop at; but the State has seen fit to back up the water in Sixth and Seventh Lakes with a dam ten feet high; the gate had just been raised "by order," and the pent-up waters were rushing downward to the Black River, to turn mill-wheels and swell the profits of some manufacturer or corporation having influence at Albany.

Making the three-quarter mile carry from Fifth to Sixth, I landed at the dam and rested for a time to take in the desolate scene.

The water at and above the dam was clogged with rotting vegetation, slimy tree-tops, and decayed, half-sunken logs. The shoreline of trees stood dead and dying, while the smell of decaying vegetable matter was sickening. Last season Sixth Lake, though small (fifty-three acres), was a wild, gamy place, and the best of the chain for floating. Its glory has departed. None care to stop there longer than is necessary. Seventh Lake, containing 1,609 acres, is the second largest lake of the chain and lies but a trifle higher than Sixth. There is no rapid water and no carry between the two, and a dam that raises the water eight or nine feet in the Sixth will raise it almost as high in the Seventh. The channel up to Seventh was as plain as a highway last year, and pleasant withal. The present season finds the channel wiped out, the forest of balsam, spruce and hemlock converted into a dismal swamp of dying trees, foul, discolored waters, and fouler smells; while the channel has puzzled more than one guide who had been used to the route for years.

However, by the help of a few blazed trees and fallen timber, with short sections cut out of the trunks for the passage of boats, I contrived to keep the channel and debouched into the once pleasant Seventh, only to find it a scene of desolation and decay. All along the shores the timber was dead or dying; and the odor of rotting vegetation was not suggestive of "ozone," or balsam-laden breezes.

As you enter the Seventh by the outlet, turn to port, follow the shore for one hundred rods, and you will find an open, free-for-all bark camp. It has been there for many years, and many are the names and dates carved on the square logs of which the sides are built. I expected to find Sam Dunakin, with Dr. Nott and party here, but they had left, though their fire was still burning. So I stopped for a rest and dinner. Across the lake, looking by the high rocky point, you could see, last season, a white, long strip of clean sand beach. Just back of the beach was a hedge-like row of green shrubbery, some fifty yards long, and just here came in the stream of Eighth Lake—the inlet of Seventh.

This, too, is all changed. Beach, hedge and inlet are all drowned out, and the dense forest, for a long distance, is under water on either side. This is bad, for the open spaces among the trees are easily mistaken for the inlet by a stranger, while the tortuous channel is hard to follow and the landing still more difficult to find. And thereby I came to grief; for, taking an after-dinner nap, I must have slept too long. The afternoon was cloudy, and my watch, that very useful companion of the lone tourist, had got wet, and, though keeping up a feeble semblance of life, had become utterly reckless as to any proper division of hours and minutes. The hands pointed to half-past two. The hands lied.

Probably it was nearer half-past five when I paddled leisurely across Seventh Lake, and, after losing half an hour looking for the inlet, started up the channel all right. I ought to have found the landing in less than one and a half miles, but I went on and on until the roar of the rapids admonished that I had gone too far upstream. Also, I had lost the marked trees which the guides had blazed to indicate the route. So I turned and paddled back, looking carefully for some sign of the landing. None was to be seen.

I skirted along the north shore, as near it as I could get, and got into a fearful mess of dead logs, submerged tree-tops and sunken brush, but no landing. All at once darkness shut down on this miserable, dismal forest like a wet blanket. A heavy black cloud showed in the southwest, and thunder began to growl ominously. And now for the open channel; for any place where dry ground may be found, with a chance to put up the shelter tent. Too late. One end of the canoe was fast on a floating log, and the first attempt to back off resulted in sticking the other end in a scraggy treetop, while the log stuck tighter than a brother.

It began to look like an uncomfortable scrape. The canoe was hung up, stem and stern, and the furious gust that usually precedes a thunder storm was roaring through the forest, tipping a balsam or spruce over here and there, making one feel uneasy as they plashed into the muddy water, their loosened roots making them an easy prey to the wind. On the heel of the wind came the rain, and how it *did* pour; while the lightning was almost incessant, and the thunder was highly creditable for a country with so few advantages.

I unjointed the paddle, and, using the single blade, got free of that execrable log. Then I worked free of the old tree-top, and, aided by the flashes that lighted the whole forest momentarily, got out into clear water, but quite idiotic as to the points of the compass. So, as there seemed nothing better to do, I sat still and watched the strange, wild scenery, as shown in different colors by electricity. There were white flashes that appeared to dash all over the forest in a broad, white glare of light, with no distinctive point of stroke. Pale-blue, zig-zag chains that gave a peculiar ghastly light among trunks and limbs, and orange colored bolts that seemed to my eye like round globes of fire. These last struck twice within a short distance of the canoe—once, a tree that stood in the water, and once on dry land. I could tell by the sound of the shattered tops, as they plashed into the water or clattered to the ground. Comfortless as the situation was, it was a grand display, also—a little unearthly and a trifle scary. It was some satisfaction to reflect that I was insured in two companies, and a random bolt or a tumbling tree might be worth three thousand dollars to the widow.

The storm lasted an unconscionable time, but was followed by a bright, clear night, and when I had made out the north star, I slowly worked down the channel, got into the lake, and made the camp again just as the eastern sky began to show streaks of light. There was plenty of dry kindling wood in the camp, and a roaring fire was in order, with a pint of strong, hot tea, broiled pork, bread and potatoes. Thanks to the waterproof shelter-tent, I was capable of a dry blanket, shirt and drawers, so, hanging my wet clothes to dry by the fire, I swathed myself snugly in blanket and tent, lay down on fragrant browse, and slept the sleep of the just man.

It is not to be supposed that a man far on the wrong side of fifty years can take an all-night soaking in a wicked storm, seated in a sixteen-pound canoe, where to rise, or even turn around, may mean drowning—can turn out, after needed sleep, with a general disposition to throw hand-springs, or perform feats of muscular agility. I awoke at about 10 a.m. on the morning of July 30, lame and sore, unwound myself from blanket and oiled shelter-tent, took a wash, built a huge fire, made some strong coffee, and tried my best to make a cheery thing of it.

It wouldn't do. The miserable dead-line of timber was about the only cheerful outlook; it was a long distance either way to human habitation or to human sympathy, and—I was just mad. I limped down to the soddened beach, sat down on a soaked log, and "nursed my wrath to keep it warm." I cursed the weak, selfish policy (if it deserves the name) that is turning the finest sylvan region on the face of the earth into a disgusting, malarial nuisance. I cursed the miserable, illogical hoodlums, who, from high positions, sing the praises of the Adirondacks as a finer, more romantic land than the Swiss Alps; begging that it be kept as a "State Park"—"an inheritance for our children's children," while, from the other corners of their mouths, they explain how the waters that, by nature, seek the St. Lawrence, may be dammed, backed up and turned, to flow into the Hudson. (See Verplanck Colvin's Reports, which I have before me.) Now, let any man, with as much brains as a hen-turkey, look over Colvin's Reports and say what the result will be if his suggestions are ever practically carried to their consummation.

But enough for the present. "An' if the beast an' branks be spared" I will ventilate this subject by another year, quite to the satisfaction of all those who advocate the damming of lakes and rivers, regardless of health, recreation and the preservation of a region the like of which does not exist on the surface of this globed earth. More anon.

Forest and Stream, Dec. 29, 1881

The 30th of last July was a bright day along the Fulton Chain, clear and cloudless. The shelter tent and blanket were made into a snug roll, the canoe lay hidden from the heat in the shade of a thicket, and everything was ready for a trip over to Raquette Lake, when two sharp-stemmed Long-Lakers darted from the outlet into the placid Seventh, and I recognized "Slim Jim" and Fred Rivett, with parties, bound to the eastern side. Seeing me on the shore they came to a halt, and Jim sang out, "Come on, Uncle Nessmuk, go through with us to Raquette."

"You'll outrow me. I'll get left."

"No, we'll keep company; come along," said Jim.

"Can you wait five minutes?" I asked.

"Yes, fifteen of them," answered Fred.

"These gentlemen would like to see your canoe work; come on," said Jim.

It struck me that the guides had got the idea. They had been at it all the season and knew just where to strike the landing that had eluded me the evening before. So I launched out and soon laid them alongside. The gentleman who headed the party was much interested and pleased with the canoe. He asked many questions and was a little skeptical about her weight, and the three youngsters who composed the balance of the party were enthusiastic. Their questions "little meaning, little relevancy bore," but the guides made some queries with meaning in them. For instance, Fred asked, as he leisurely picked up his oars, "Did the storm keep you awake last night?" And I, remembering that my little hatchet had gone on to the Raquette, answered stoutly, "Not a bit; never slept better in my life."

As the guides took up the easy, effective stroke that sends the Long-Lakers through the water so speedily, I crept under Fred's counter, took the draw of his wake, and made the inlet without parting company. Then I said, "Boys, your boats can and ought to beat any paddle on open water, but when you come to these crooked channels, outlets and inlets in the form of the letter 'S,' where you have to look over your shoulders right and left to see the course and pull first to starboard, then to port, why you see the paddle—the double blade—has rather got the bulge on you." We had stopped under a huge cedar for a modest nip, for which the leader of that party has my thanks, and, as Jim and Fred very quietly resumed their oars, a meaning glance passed between them. They said nothing; but I thought it as well to lay aside extra clothing, spit on my hands and settle down to work.

For the first half-mile the odds were rather in my

favor. The water was deep, channel crooked and the chances for cutting off bends and "going as you look" rather made an easy thing of it. Then the course grew straighter and less distinct. The swift Long-Lakers drew rapidly away, and I saw them turn a bend forty rods ahead. I tried to cut off the bend and ran onto a sunken log. Backed off, took the channel and put on all the steam I had at command, but in vain. I was left. I paddled up the stream until I lost the blazed trees which marked the course, stopped, listened a moment, and then used my spare wind in a loud, long la-whoop. An answer came from the swampy forest far to the left, where I found the party landed up on a shaky sort of corduroy platform, which is the landing now. They were waiting for me, they said. And Fred remarked, "A double blade *does* take the skates on these crooked channels. Notice how he cut the corners and went the way he looked?" Boys, I hope that wasn't "sarkasm." I have faith to think you wouldn't make fun of grayhairs!

I like to see the guides organize for a "carry," and I watched Jim and Fred as they prepared for the trip over to Eighth Lake. First, the "party" was loaded up with fishing rods, guns, packbaskets, gum blankets and the usual impedimenta of the average tourist, and started over the carry looking like a crew of pack-peddlers. When they were out of sight, Jim remarked coolly, "We can take it easy; they ain't going to hurry." Then he and Fred tied in oars, seats, etc., snugly and neatly, made the neck-yokes fast at the balancing point, and then, inverting the lightest boat, Jim held the stern high in the air while Fred crept under and adjusted the neck-yoke nicely to his muscular shoulders, saying, "All right; let go," which Jim did; and the inevitable blue boat, with a pair of sturdy legs beneath, disappeared rapidly up the trail.

Jim raised his own boat and said, "Think you can hold her up?" I thought I could and did, though balancing on a point at the stern, and weighing over ninety pounds, she was a lift. And then Jim quietly seized my blanket roll and hung it on his broad shoulders without comment before shouldering his boat. It was a kindly thing to do and like his generous nature; but I was ashamed and raised a feeble remonstrance; he went away with a long, quick stride, paying no heed, and I thought of honest old Jack Falstaff, that Prince of Dead-beats—"Hal, an thou seest me down in the fight and bestride me, why so; 'tis an act of friendship." Was I a beat?

I organized my own canoe for the carry and tried to overtake the party, but the guides walk fast. I found them on the clean, sandy landing; and it was a relief to see the fresh green shores, wholesome waters and healthy trees of Eighth Lake, after an experience of Fifth, Sixth and Seventh. At the Eighth the leader of the party began to feel hurried. He wished to reach Bennett's Landing on Raquette in time for the little steamer to Blue Mountain, and guides always follow the wishes of employers so far as they can. I saw I was likely to get left; but, meaning to keep up as far as possible, I paddled out with the party and rather got down on the double blade. The guides went in for an ash breeze. The distance is less than one and one-half miles, and they led me to the landing just about one hundred rods. Yes, the Long-Lakers *are* fast— but cranky and uncomfortable to ride in.

As you strike the landing at the head of Eighth Lake, there is a path, leading along the shore to the right, which leads you to a cool spring. Here the guides, having seen the party off, stopped a few minutes for a lunch. Let me commend that spring, with its bright, cold water and restful surroundings, to any lone canoeist who may happen to strike the landing at the head of Eighth Lake. Again the boats and canoe were shouldered, Jim, as before, toting my blanket roll. Again the guides beat me over the carry, though they stopped for a rest and I did not— and when I arrived at Brown's Tract Inlet, guides and boats had disappeared. I was in no hurry. The carries were all made, and six and a half miles of paddling lay between me and Ed Bennett's. The day was fine. The wind just brisk enough to be lively, and I reached Bennett's about three-quarters of an hour behind the guides.

Going down the inlet, I was interested by the movements of the fish that lay basking near the surface among the lily pads, and darted off with a plash and swirl as the canoe neared them. A man with oars would hardly have seen this. But, paddling silently down stream, looking the way I went, I probably started more than a score of good-sized fish, without being able to decide on the species. I intended to return and try them, both with fly and bait, but failed to do so; though I certainly shall if I find myself there in the summer of '82. I thought they might be pickerel, but the guides assured me there were no pickerel in Raquette Lake.

I found Bennett's hotel crowded with tourists and sportsmen and was unable to get a room, or even a bed. But the bark-roofed guide camp, "For guides only," had a bright fire in front, with balsam browse for bedding, and was preferable to a close room. I took up my quarters there while on the Raquette and had no cause to regret it. As to the fare, whoever has stayed with Ed Bennett knows that his table would rank as first-class anywhere. And there is no pleasanter lake than Raquette in the North Woods. It is the largest; the water is clear, and the shores, while being well wooded, are mainly rocky. Large as the lake is, I should not know where to paddle to get more than a mile from the nearest land. The numberless bays, capes, indentations and islands make it difficult to describe on paper, and even the best maps fail to give just the correct idea of it.

I do not know a better place to investigate the now popular bass question. In the summer of '80 the small-mouth had got a pretty strong fin-hold and was evidently making his way. A few were being taken with spoon and bait. His increase for the next twelve months was to me marvelous. Starting from Bennett's landing with an hour's sun and paddling to the mouth of the Marion, I could get all the sport I wanted and more fish than I needed before dark. I used an eight-ounce rod and the scarlet ibis fly with silver body, as the best. But a brown hackle was also killing. And the gold-bodied ibis is about as good. The three, taken as a cast, and no others are needed.

Father Gavan, an intelligent young Catholic priest, was an enthusiastic bass fisherman, and used a powerful rod with minnow or spoon. His favorite ground was the mouth of South Inlet and adjacent shores. He was nearly always successful. I liked the mouth of the Marion and the rocky shores below, with the islands in front of the hotel. There was not much to choose. His fish averaged about twice the size of mine, and I could take about two to his one. On the whole, I should say that the bait fisherman had the best of it. The guides' complaint, that the bass has destroyed all the lake trout, would have more point had there been any lake trout worth mention to destroy.

I took a lively interest in the tourists, or boarders, who had worked their way into the wilderness for health and not for sport. There were many of them on the waters of the Raquette and more on the Saranacs. News travels fast in the woods. Every day that I was on these waters I saw guides and tourists from almost every route you can mention. I heard that more than a dozen consumptives had already died on the Saranac waters. Others were dying, and many more had crept away, beaten and exhausted, to die at home among friends and relatives.

Paul Smith had said he would, by five hundred dollars, rather the article entitled "Camp Lou" had never been written. I saw for myself that parties who had sought the Adirondacks for health were sick, disgusted, and only anxious to get away anywhere that dryness, warmth, and rest were easily attainable. I was interviewed and questioned time and again as to the healthfulness of the mountainous regions about the headwaters of the Susquehanna; and truth compelled me to say that all my observation and experience led to the conclusion that the high lands about the headwaters of the Delaware and Susquehanna afforded more hope of healing to the sufferer from pulmonary disease than the damp, cold high lands of the Northern Wilderness. That some unexpected and surprising cures have happened in both regions is certainly true.

And it is equally true that the Northern Wilderness is unrivalled for boating and canoeing facilities and hardly to be excelled for scenery. All this is most attractive, and it is not to be wondered at that the average tourist much prefers a wild region, where, by making short carries, he can travel hundreds of miles by water.

But, as regards the single question of health, I can name half a dozen localities, easily reached in one day from New York, where I would rather take my chances as a consumptive patient than in the Adirondack region. [A paragraph of digression is omitted here.]

At Raquette Lake I met Mr. Durant, in whose boat my knapsack had gone off. I accosted him; and before I could make any inquiries he smiled and said, "I guess I know what you are going to say. Your knapsack is over at my camp. You can get it in two minutes." I found the camp a well-furnished summer residence, and the genial proprietor quite capable of keeping not only guides and boats, but a neat little steam yacht. Money is a good thing—when one knows how to use it. I found the knapsack all right, to the last fishhook, and was more than glad to get it. When I had it well packed with blanket, shelter tent, hatchet, tinware, etc., I felt at home again and went over to Leavitt's on Forked Lake, bound down the Raquette River, and—just where the notion might take me.

At Leavitt's I found some guides whom I knew the previous season and got some useful notes and points on routes, carries, etc. Also met the Justice of the Peace who issued the warrant for Charles Parker, the man who caused such a scandal in the Long Lake region last summer. I gave a summary of that unhappy affair in *Forest and Stream* last August, and it is pretty well understood now that it throws no stigma on the "guide class." [In the summer of 1880 one Charles Parker, said to be an itinerant laborer rather than a qualified guide and a comparative stranger to the Long Lake neighborhood, was hired as a guide by a woman tourist. She accused Parker of attacking her. A warrant for his arrest was issued at Long Lake. He was traced to Kingston, Ontario, extradited, and brought back to Long Lake for trial; he again escaped and was later found hiding near Forked Lake in company with friends. He resisted the peace officer sent to arrest him and was shot in the resultant melee. The affair created a furore. The public press took up the case, and one New York paper in particular unjustly stigmatized professional guides as a class. Whereupon friends and patrons of the guides rallied to their defense—and printer's ink flew in both directions. Nessmuk wrote a vigorous defense of the guides in a letter to *Forest and Stream,* published Aug. 18, 1881. This is the letter referred to.]

Forked Lake is one of the most beautiful sheets of water in the wilderness, and a healthy, delightful region for a summer camp, of which there are several on eligible points — well-furnished summer residences owned by men of taste, wealth and leisure, who have the good sense to take their families to the forest for three months or more, rather than to such resorts as Long Branch, Newport, etc. It is possibly quite as expensive; but, I should say, worth the cost.

It was a most delightful morning in August. I got an early breakfast and launched out for Long Lake, intending to stop awhile with Mitchell Sabattis and investigate the fish question, of which I had heard a good deal in connection with this fine sheet of water. It is said that two guides who had been prosecuted for crusting deer stocked the lake with pickerel out of revenge, and that the pickerel have exterminated the salmon trout. And now there are black bass in the lake, which, in turn, are demolishing the pickerel. Such is the tale as it was told to me.

I doubt it. I do not believe that any fresh water fish can exterminate the agile, sharp-nosed pickerel. Though it is fair to add the testimony of Mr. E. Rose, who has a fine summer resort on Silver Lake, Susquehanna County, Pa., and is a life-long sportsman. Pickerel were certainly plenty in that lake twelve years ago. The lake was stocked with small-mouthed bass, and now he assures me the pickerel are gone. The bass have cleaned them out. Maybe. I dunno; I dunno. I cannot believe that the small-mouth whips the pickerel in fight. But he may starve him out.

From Leavitt's to the outlet of Forked Lake are four miles of as pretty water and scenery as a tourist could ask. If you are a canoeist don't swing over to port for the sake of an open channel. Keep near the right shore, and when you open the course to the outlet you may have a mile or so of heavy paddling among the lily-pads, but you will cut off considerable distance, and the double-blade works in lily-pads, while oars tangle up. You will be interested, too, in seeing at every open space fair sized fish drop away from the canoe, leaving a funnel-shaped swirl on the surface, and you will be puzzled, as I was, to name the fish. I am sorry I did not put the rod together and try them with the fly; but I promised myself to do that when I came back.

When you reach the landing at the outlet take the

double-blade apart, turn the stems to the ends of the
canoe, tie them fast, organize your duffle for the carry,
and then spend an hour following along the bank and
taking in the rapids, with the scenery on either side. If
you have an eye for nature, the time will not be lost. The
carry is one and a half miles, and a man who lives there
will drag your canoe across for a dollar and a half. As
you can carry it in thirty minutes more safely, you had
better trust your own shoulders.

As you reach the foot of the carry you launch again
for an east trip of one and a half miles; another and a
shorter carry, then a half-mile by water, then a carry of
one hundred rods, and you strike the head of Long Lake.
It is four miles to the landing at Kellog's and a little less
to Mitchell Sabattis' landing. To make the latter you
turn to the right on sighting the bridge at Kellog's and
steer to the right end of the sandy beach before you. Take
the steep path that leads up from the landing, and Auntie
Sabattis will take care of you. She has been doing that
sort of thing for a good many years. What the famous
Indian guide, Mitchell Sabattis [see plates XVII and
XVIII], is in the woods, his wife can supplement him as
camp-keeper.

I found no tourists at the Sabattis house, but it was not
lonely. Two married daughters, a son and his wife, with
eight grandchildren pretty nearly of one size, made it
quite lively for Grandma Sabattis. She managed the
household well and kept the unruly youngsters in order
to a degree that won my admiration. I was glad to meet
the son, Ike Sabattis, whose acquaintance I had made
in the summer of '80, and was sorry that Mitchell was
away guiding.

I should have been pleased to meet Ike's suggestion that we go down Long Lake floating; but, alas, we were both on the sick list. Ike was suffering from a severe attack of cholera morbis, and I had been growing weaker every day since leaving the Forge House. I coughed almost incessantly and had sweating spells every night. I lost appetite. My knees jackknifed going over the shortest carries, and I began to realize that I might get laid by the heels in the middle of the wilderness, hundreds of miles away from home. I have little feeling for myself or any other man, as a sick patient. But no man can transcend possibilities, and, as it happens, sickness does come to us all, soon or late.

The muscular young guide, Ike Sabattis, was on his back. Two other young guides, Hall and Staunton, were far gone with consumption, the latter in a dying condition at the Long Lake settlement. All the same, I was ashamed of the physical weakness that steadily headed me off from day to day and did my best to beat it, but in vain. I kept my feet, however; fished, excursed in the woods, paddled down to Kellog's every day and picked up all the information possible.

Not a day passed that I did not hear of a death in the Saranac region from consumption. Landlords and guides looked serious at these reports, but did not dispute them. They said, "These people were past help when they came in. They should have stayed at home." Perhaps; but it does not go to prove that a residence in the North Woods is a cure for lung diseases.

It was on the sand beach in front of Kellog's that I met a young invalid of the feminine persuasion who interested me more deeply than any human being had ever done on so short an acquaintance.

It was a perfect morning. The lake was like a mirror. I had paddled down without particular aim or object, and was drawing the canoe up the beach when I noticed a little girl walking with cat-like tread up and down the shore and humming an opera catch softly to herself.

Suddenly she stepped up to the canoe, raised it by the stem, turned it to port and starboard, read the name, and said sharply, "Humph! 'Susan Nipper.' Dickens. 'Master Dombey is a permanency; Miss Edith is temporary.' Why don't you name her Miss Edith? She looks sufficiently temporary."

She was about the first one who had recognized the name, and I looked her over with more interest. Why, she was a woman! Hair and eyes like an Indian princess—weight and size like a girl of ten years. A thin, attenuated form, a bright glow in either cheek, and a sharp, intellectual expression, with the worn, womanly outlines, told the story. She pushed the canoe afloat, drew it back and forth, hauled it up on the beach, and said in a low, sad voice, "Oh, I should *so* like a ride in it—would you dare let me?"

"Dare? My dear young lady, can you trust yourself?"

"I am used to boats and water; we have a guide and a good boat," she answered, "but I would like to ride in this."

So I took the old handkerchief with its stuffing of hemlock browse and ferns that serves me for a seat, placed it well forward, made the shelter-tent and blanket into a comfortable lean-back in the bow, and seated her as I would an infant. Got in carefully myself, with the old grass coat between the keelson and the terminus of my spinal column, and paddled cautiously up and down the shore in three feet of water to test her seagoing qualities. She was steady and immovable as a sandbag.

Then she said: "You see I am safe? Now cross the lake and land me in the woods."

I did. When we were more than half way across there came a loud "*halloo*" from the landing. She opened her large black eyes, waved her sailor hat and settled back, saying: "It's my father. He will understand."

I landed her on the beach just where the firs and spruce were thickest, spread tent and blanket on a dry sunny spot and left her to herself. For an hour she reclined on the improvised couch or gathered the trifling ferns and lichens of which young ladies are so fond, and then she said, quite as though I had been her guide: "Now take me back to my father. I am tired—*so* tired." So I landed her on the clean, white beach where *pater familias* was impatiently poking the sand with his gold-headed cane, and resigned my position as amateur guide. She held out her thin little hand at parting, saying: "I trust you will understand me? I am a dying girl. They let me do as I please now. I have left conventional fetters and forms behind, with a good deal more that I valued once —but no matter. Good-bye." Was there a little romance connected with her case, I wonder?

As the old gentleman seemed nervous, I thought it a good time to leave, and went up to the village to call on Ike Sabattis. Found him much better and disposed to go down the lake floating. Thought he could "put me on to a deer." But the man who is liable to a hard coughing spell at a minute's notice is more likely to scare three deer than to get a shot at one, so I declined, and paddled around the point to the grove near Sabattis' landing, where I spent hours sitting on a log—a style of amusement in which I was fast becoming an adept—bidding fair to rival "Old Phelps." Indeed, it was getting to be my "best hold."

And here while listlessly watching the calm, clear water, I witnessed one of the little incidents that the lone tourist who knows the value of silence may often pick up. It was only a couple of little fish; a bull-head four or five inches long and a bass much smaller. The former was working his way laboriously along the beach, his nose at the surface and his rudder gone, while the bass was spitefully nipping him at the counter. It was evidently a hopeless case for the bull-head; and such a piece of uncalled for cussedness on the part of the bass that, unthinkingly, I seized a stick of flood-trash and made a vicious clip at him. As often happens in this world, the innocent suffered while the guilty rascal "lit out" for deep water. May he grow to a four-pounder, to be worried and tormented along that same beach, with a sharp hook in his gills.

(The continuation of Nessmuk's narrative, detailing the further incidents of his story at Mitchell Sabattis', forms a stirring story of Adirondack life. It is given below. Editor, *Forest and Stream*)

A Night Race Against Death

After dark, as I was smoking by Auntie Sabattis' gate, two brisk-stepping young guides came hurriedly by through the yard and made for the landing below the hill. They carried a sharp-stemmed Long-Laker and a lantern. They were bound on a night trip to Raquette Lake and return, to be back before sunrise; for young Staunton, the sick guide, lay dying, and his one wish was to see and know a favorite brother before crossing the Dark Carry. And the doctor had said that, if the brothers were to know each other again on earth, the meeting must take place before another sunrise.

It was rather a manly, plucky thing to make a night cruise of between thirty and forty miles, mostly in a fog, and with four carries, two stretches of rocky, tortuous current and two lakes, all to be "doubled" in the darkness. The lantern would only be available on the carries. On water the course is better seen without it. I followed the guides to the landing and watched them with interest as, bending to oar and paddle, they disappeared swiftly into the darkness.

Then I went up to the house, consumed the time cutting up plug and smoking it, tried to feel at ease; but the dying guide and absent brother somehow got in on my nerves. I mentioned that I would like to know just how the sick man was getting on; if he was likely to pull through the night.

"You'll know," said Auntie Sabattis; "when anyone dies here, the bell is tolled as soon as anyone can get to it, night or day."

I went to my room. The night was very warm, and I was unwell and weak. I am not nervous. I have no sympathy or pity for nerves—my own or others'. But how the dread of that bell did worry me. I pictured to myself the guides racing over the course in the foggy summer night, going quickly over the slippery carries, one carrying the boat, the other lighting the path with glimmering lantern; rowing swiftly across long stretches of water by the shimmer and glitter of starlight; reaching the camp on an island in Raquette Lake, only to find George Staunton gone off, floating with his "party."

I thought of the "ride from Ghent to Aix," but that race was on horseback. The strain of muscle came heaviest on "Roland." Here, the Roland was a cranky, narrow Long-Laker, and the muscle was of men. Would they win? I walked the room, smoked and listened. A stroke of that bell would have made me stagger like a drunken man. But it came not.

At midnight I turned in for a few hours of drowsy, feverish unrest, and at 3 a.m. I dressed and walked down to the landing, where I made a fire against the rock used as a washing station by the House of Sabattis, lighted a pipe and resumed my favorite exercise of sitting on a log. The fog still hung over the lake, thick and dark.

Then came faint, dull streaks of light, gray and brown, from the east. It grew lighter; gray and brown turned to dull yellow. "Owl's Head" began to be visible. The fog grew denser, brighter, and began to rise in well-defined lines from off the water, like the lifting of a blanket; and from under the blanket darted a sharp-stemmed regulation Long-Laker, the same oars and paddle playing with unabated vim, but with three men instead of two.

She came to the landing with a swift, silent rush, and, before she was fairly still, an athletic young man sprang to the beach and took his way through the grove toward the settlement at a seven-knot gait. I had no need to ask if it were George Staunton. It was less than a half-mile from the landing to where his brother lay dying.

Now, suppose, just as he came in sight of the house where his brother lay that the bell should give his nerves a trial with its first, fearful, death-announcing clang! Would he stagger some? Would he sort o' swerve off to port and sit down on a log, faint, and white and sick? It might be. It was painful. I took out my watch as he disappeared in the grove. I said, "He will be there in five minutes." The minutes passed. One guide said, "How long?" "Six minutes," I answered. "Six minutes is enough to get there," he said. I still held the watch. Ten minutes passed. "He is there," I said; "has been there five minutes." Then the guides tied in oars, paddle and seats, took up lantern and boat and started for the little hamlet, called on the maps "Long Lake P. O."

I never did and never shall like the Long-Lakers. They are swift but frail, weak, cranky and tiresome to ride in. Nevertheless, as the fagged guides brushed past me I instinctively raised my old felt hat to the craft that had run an all-night race against death—and won.

Forest and Stream, April 13, 1882

Whoever makes a lone cruise in a light canoe through the Adirondacks will be nearly certain to take in Long Lake. He can hardly avoid it. He will do well to give to it as much time and attention as he can afford. No one tourist can even approximately go over what I may call the Long Lake region in a three months' cruise. There are more than fifty snug nooks and camping spots on the shores of the lake proper. There are twelve small lakes and ponds easily reached by easy carries from the main lake. The quiet, shady, peaceful, lonely retreats that may be picked up and occupied by the way-wise tourist are beyond computation. It is true there is a settlement, a hotel and a post office on the west shore of the lake. Also, a road. But an hour's paddling takes you quite away from civilization. You can choose your ground where to camp and be utterly alone for a month, or an entire season, if you choose.

Paddling across the lake from Kellog's, one half mile brings you to the inlet of Clear Pond [now Lake Eaton]. About the mouth is grand fishing for pickerel. A little more than a half mile below is the mouth of Big Brook, also an excellent fishing ground for pickerel, and you may take the much despised but toothsome bullhead, or catty, in plenty. You may go up either of these streams, with a few carries, to Little Tupper Lake, going through Mud Pond, Little Slim and Slim Ponds, with Stony Pond at last. And all the way you may select camping grounds that ought to more than satisfy any man who is seeking healthful rest and sylvan life.

I had formed an adverse opinion of Long Lake. I had thought it too civilized. Too many guides. Too much landlordism. Too much cost for the accommodations. Every day that I was on Long Lake, the hotel detailed employees to go around the village with guests, to quarter them in private houses. Why so few of them found quarters at the old and time-honored house of Sabattis was because the house of Sabattis was too prolific of young half-breeds. There were nine of them when I was there. One little blue-eyed fiend, as white as a Saxon, ran altogether to fight. He would pitch into his half-brother —a fine, pleasant, bright-eyed half-breed—with teeth, nails and fists, without a sign of provocation. I got tired of seeing it. I said to the strong, muscular, dusky, dark-eyed descendant of the house of Sabattis, "Cuff him up to a peak and knock the peak off." And he did it. Auntie Sabattis came around and I explained. She gathered a yearling plum sprout, and I hope the lacing that vicious little imp got then and there will last him awhile.

It was on a bright August morning that I paddled across the lake from Kellog's, with a notion of going to Little Tupper, via Clear Pond, etc. I had heard all the guides' stories about the introduction of pickerel to Long Lake. How Lysander Hall and a guide by the name of Shaw had been prosecuted for crusting deer, and in revenge, had brought pickerel from the "eastern side." If so—and I think it is—they "builded better than they knew." At that time the lake trout were almost a myth. Today I can take more pickerel and other toothsome fish than a camp of six hearty men can eat from day to day.

Now, my sporting friends, will you heed a little logic from the standpoint of fifty years' experience? You work eleven months in the twelve at desk or bench. All through the year you are looking to an outing; a chance to get away for one, two or three weeks' vacation. You know, and I know, and we all know, that you need it and deserve it. But why in the name of all sense and reason should you boast of "bags" and "baskets"? About how much, on an average, do you require as animal food? Say, in twenty-four hours? If you kill more, why and wherefore? The man who brags to me of "bags" and "baskets" just tempts me to "shoot him on the spot."

With my hand on my mouth, and my mouth in the dust, I admit that I shot thirty-six deer in a season. I deserved to be hung for it. Again, in Eaton County, Michigan, I killed seventeen deer. With these exceptions, I

have never killed more than ten or twelve yearly. And
yet my conscience squirms. Why should I ever have killed
a deer that I did not need for immediate use? Why, in
the name of heaven, was I looking for market prices and
quotations? Well, I was young. I knew no better. Today, the mother doe or the spotted fawn can pass me on
a runway as safely as my own mother.

Last summer, among the duffle that I took into the
North Woods, was my favorite single-barreled, hair-
triggered rifle. With it I have driven the nail five times
in succession at the distance of one hundred feet. At one
hundred yards the deer would be lucky that got away
from me with a standing shot. Now, when the season
opened, I could have had an open standing shot any
morning when I chose to seek it.

I took in just twelve bullets.

I brought the entire twelve home again. I did not load
the rifle once last summer. There was no occasion. At
Mr. Lamberton's camp, at Ed Arnold's, at the Pratt
camp, at Sam Dunakin's, and other places, I could get
a piece of venison when I needed it. What earthly excuse
had I for sending a bullet crashing through the bones
and quivering flesh of a bright-eyed, graceful denizen of
the woods? And so the old rifle rests by the ingle-lug,
and I only take it out once a month to keep my shooting
up in offhand practice, which is, after all, the only rifle
practice worth talking about.

And just here and now I want to put in my oar on offhand shooting. Offhand shooting is not done by sticking
a hickory wiping rod in your left pocket, extending the
other end, and gripping rod and barrel together to steady
the hand. It is not done by twisting your body out of all

grace and comeliness to get a "hiprest." It is done by taking a firm, free stand on both feet, drawing the rifle to a graceful and natural position, with both elbows free of the body, getting the best bead you can, and cutting loose at the right instant. That is offhand shooting. As for all rests, they are well enough in sighting a gun, but once sure that your sights are plumb center, take no more resting shots. It may be good civil engineering, but is unworthy the notice of American riflemen. This is by way of digression.

At the mouth of Big Brook I tried the pickerel, with light tackle and an eight-ounce rod. With a two-oared skiff and strong tackle I would have lain just inside the lily-pads and cast outside into clear water. With a sixteen pound canoe and a light trout rig I thought it wiser to lie off about forty feet in clear water and cast toward the thick mass of lily-pads, hoping to stop any fellow I might hook before he could get into a bad tangle among the lily stems. It worked very well at the start. A lively, bright-sided little fellow of a pound and a half took the lure handsomely, almost at the first cast, and got the canoe to the fringe of lily leaves that covered the water like a carpet before I could get him in. I laid off again and soon had the mate to him. The sport was fine. I began to wake up. Paddling up a few rods, off the deepest part of the inlet, I began to cast with a bigger bait and deeper trolling.

And then and there I saw a huge pickerel driving straight at the lure and in the morning light showing distinctly as though lying on the beach. I might easily have jerked the hooks away and saved my rod; but I was in the humor for a racket, so let him snap his huge, sharky jaws over hooks, bait, and more than half the strong wire snell, which he did, and turned with a heavy swirl for his mysterious cavern among the lily roots. I gave him the butt (I think that is the correct term), and the brave old rod took the form of a loop for a few seconds, then the top joint broke down to a right angle, the canoe commenced a lively waltz into the lily-pads, and the next minute I was sitting in the canoe holding a line in my hand that ran to the bottom—straight up and down—the broken rod dragging overboard, and a wrathy angler trying to raise a big pickerel by the handline dodge. It didn't work well. Somehow he seemed to have collateral security on the heavy toad-lily roots at the bottom. First he would creep slowly away with a yard or two of line; then I would as slowly get it back inch by inch. I gathered loose line, got a long bight and passed it under a rib of the canoe, hauled taut and making all fast. Took in the old rod, filled a pipe, and made a "dead set" at patience.

Once, under similar conditions, I saved a twenty-two pound maskalonge in High Bank Lake, Michigan. I thought I might tire out this fellow, but he was not to be had. I spoke of light tackle. The rod was light, made by Heyling of Rochester. It was a beauty in '60; in '82 it may have been a little dull and dead. The line was the taper, waterproof, in common use at present. The wire snell and hooks had been tested at forty-four pounds. For two mortal hours I sat in that eggshell, trying all sorts of dodges to start my customer. Then my patience went by the board. I seized the line and got down on muscle. Something gave way. It was the line. What would he weigh? Perhaps twelve pounds; certainly more than eight. He weighed enough to wreck my tackle and rod.

I gathered and stowed the wreck of rod and line. I was not so very sorry. It was quite an experience and a partial excuse for backing down from a trip I was physically unfit for. I paddled across the placid lake to Kellog's and asked for mail. There was none. I was glad of it. No news is good news. I had a set of tin dishes that I think can hardly be beaten. They were made without handles, or wire in the rims, nesting together, and filling all requirements of boiling, frying, and baking. The old shanty tent, that had often sheltered me and a couple of friends through a rainy night, and only weighed four and one-quarter pounds, that could be put up in an emergency as quickly as I could cut a twelve foot pole— this and these I gave away, reserving a single dish in which to make coffee.

Once, I would not have believed that I could pass "Owl's Head" without ascending it to the uttermost peak. Now, I said, the view of a mountain top from the bosom of a placid lake is much finer than a view of many lakes from the top of a cold, windy, cheerless mountain.

I was getting weak—demoralized, may be. I paddled up Long Lake, took the carries slowly and wearily, and brought up at Leavitt's late in the afternoon of a model August day. Even as I went over the carries, Charles Parker, with his wife and boat, was lurking near the trail; and his Nemesis, in the person of Warren Cole, was also on his very heels. When Parker launched his boat at the second carry, Cole was there and ordered a halt. Parker dodged behind his wife and tried to get off. Cole shot him. The public know the rest.

Going up the carries, I was passed by two guides with their boats and parties. One of them carried a boat that struck me as being the best guide boat of the Long Lake model I had seen in the North Woods. It would carry three persons with baggage, was finished in oil and varnish, and weighed forty-eight pounds. Had it been put together with white cedar strips instead of pine, and oval, red elm ribs one and a half inches apart, instead of clumsy spruce knees six or seven inches apart, it would have been nearly perfection as a guide boat.

There was a crowd at Leavitt's, on Forked Lake, and, crossing Raquette Lake to Ed Bennett's, I found the hotel full to overflowing, the overflow finding sleeping quarters in open bark camps. It suited me. The table was excellent, as I have always found it. And an open camp with a fire in front is breezier, freer, healthier than any indoor arrangement for sleeping.

I pre-empted a corner of the "guides' camp," mended the old rod, and spent days paddling around the rocky shores of mainland and island, fly-fishing for bass. They nearly always rose to a red ibis or brown hackle, though here, in Pennsylvania, we can hardly coax the small mouth to notice a fly. With us, he runs entirely to crayfish and dobsons. I shall come to understand his various ways in various waters—about as soon as I solve the grouse problem.

It was on a bright morning in August that I let go, and started for Third Lake, leaving my dunnage, save a light knapsack, to be taken charge of by "Slim Jim," who had gone across to the Saranacs. The morning, the lake, the scenery, all would justify a younger man in a little enthusiastic description; and it was not altogether lost on me. Bass were jumping all along the rocky shores, a brace of hounds—although it was out of season—were sending the deer along the high ridge to the southward at a killing pace, and I met two guide boats with parties who had been out all night, floating. Each party had a deer, and I was pleased to see that they were both bucks. I reached Brown's Tract Inlet before the west wind commences to blow—as it does about every fair day—and, going up that very crooked stream, again saw the disappearing fish among the lily-pads, the same that had puzzled me before. But I was too weak and listless to try them without bait or fly.

Half way up the inlet I came near getting cut down by a seventeen-foot Long-Laker. She was coming down at a rapid rate, and just as I was rounding one of the numerous short bends, her sharp iron prow came in sight at steamboat speed, pointed directly at my midships. The old whaling instincts came to the surface at once. I yelled "starn-all," dropped the paddle, seized the cutwater of the threatening boat, and held her off with all my strength. The guide behaved finely. At the first sound of my voice he dipped his oars deep and backed for all the ash was worth. But she was a large boat, coming down stream under strong headway, with three men and baggage, and not to be stopped instantly. But her headway was deadened. She came on until her stem pressed heavily on the side of the frail canoe, bending it inward. I was pressed and crowded as a hare among marsh grass and bushy tangles of muddy vegetation; then she stopped, receded; the guide dipped his oars and dashed away. I was faint, but the canoe was safe. No word was spoken. But that guide has impressed me as a cool, capable fellow. Getting your canoe crushed in a lonely forest is quite as bad as being "put a-foot" on the Western plains, through losing your broncho.

Though my entire load—canoe and knapsack—was less than twenty-six pounds, the carry from the inlet to Eighth Lake was trying, in my weak state.

Alva Dunning [see plate XIX] had loaned me the key of his camp on the Eighth, and I rested there a couple of hours, taking a lunch from his stores, and leaving the key hidden at the root of a stump as agreed on. The Eighth was a beauty on that bright, warm day. There was not a human being save myself about the lake. The water, lying as nature made it, was ruffled into breezy waves, capped with white. But for the quavering cry of a solitary loon and the gentle lapping of the water on the island shore, there was no sound, and the next relay would take me to Seventh and Sixth, with backwater and dead timber lines, decaying vegetation, nauseous smells, and all the curses that come of destroying forest lakes and streams for man's selfish greed. (N.B. Does it ever occur to the average guide that he has a better moral right to explode a can of dynamite under one of these dams than a selfish monopolist has to poison the air that men, women and helpless children are forced to breathe and drink?) To say nothing of the destruction of fish, the converting of a beautiful sheet of water into a scene of desolation that will last long after the porcine instigator has rotted in his grave, and his ill-gotten gains are scattered by his pampered worthless offspring. "The evil that men do lives after them." As it ought.

Let me pass quickly over the desolate Seventh and Sixth. They were of course worse than when I cruised up the "Chain." The air at the foot of Sixth was sickening. One year before the Sixth would have been a pleasant location for an all-summer camp. At the foot of Sixth the gate was up, and a broad sheet of white, foamy water was rushing like an arrow toward the Fifth. Of course this affected the five lower lakes.

I found the camp at the foot of Fifth lowered by the rush of water, for which I was sorry, for there was heavy thunder in an ominous looking cloud in the southwest. But the distance is short between Fifth and the "Stormy Fourth," as Colvin calls it. And the outlet was rushing like a mill-tail. I jumped the canoe, and the only use I had for the paddle was in holding back and dodging dangerous obstructions.

In less than five minutes I was on Fourth Lake; and as I saw the black, whirling cloud and listened to the heavy, stunning peals, I thought it as well to put on a little extra muscle for the Pratt camp, half a mile below. As I rounded the point on which the camp is located, I saw Tom Jones and another gentlemen — stranger to me—with Dick Cragoe, their guide, sitting on the porch watching the coming storm. Dick, in accordance with North Woods etiquette, came down to "land" me, and it struck him as a good idea to also house his own boat. And hardly had we made all snug when the tornado swooped down on the lake. It was sublime.

I have been in a white squall in the tropics, in a *pampero* off the Argentine coast, and have seen the terrific electric storms of the West. But I never saw so heavy a sea kicked up on an inland lake at such short notice. In two minutes the water was dashing up the sloping landing to the door of the boat-house; sharp, steep, white-crested waves were chasing each other like racehorses; the gale tore their spumy tops off and sent them whirling to leeward in a white mist of blinding spray; tall trees a century old were seized by the hair of the head and dashed to earth, while the zig-zagging of lightning and the heavy bellowing of thunder were just the adjuncts to make the scene perfect. When the storm was at its fiercest Dig Cragoe had his hands full to free, with mop and broom, the sitting room from water that drove in under the door.

In twenty minutes the storm had howled and whirled itself away to the northeast, the sun came out warm and mellow, the air was a delight, and the lake subsided to a placid, sleepy roll as quickly as it had risen.

It was a model evening for a cruise, and the Pratt camp organized for a thirteen mile row down to the Forge House (foot of First Lake). I paddled out for Third Lake and was soon passed by the strong pull of Dick with his party. Fred Hess, another guide, came out from the Fifth, where in a thicket he had been dodging the storm. Two other guides, "Slim Jim" and Fred Rivett, overhauled me soon after. They too had been dodging under their boats in the wood between Fifth and Fourth Lakes. It was nearly dark when I halted at Ed Arnold's. His hostelry was crowded to its utmost, and his grounds were jubilant with lively parties and well-paid guides. It was pitch dark when I arrived at Perrie's on Third Lake. The camp was overrun with boarders, parties, and guides. There was not spare sleeping room for a cat. He assured me that he had been sleeping for a week on tables, chairs, trunks, any place where he could get a few hours' nightly rest. A. G. Buell, who owns the Third Lake House, had a newly made fragrant bark camp, and was alone. He invited me to stay with him during my sojourn on the lake, and divide any sport or work that might turn up. As I like cooking and he detests it, we managed to make the arrangement very satisfactory.

For a few days I fished, frogged, cooked, picked berries, climbed hill, paddled and doctored. All in vain. I grew weaker day by day. I was getting to the point where the grasshopper becomes a burden. I had sought the wilderness for health. I had lost instead of gaining. I had found many others with a similar record, and also many who claimed to have been decidedly benefited.

I had planned a cruise of 1000 miles. The log showed 206, besides many short trips not noted. I was listless, easily tired, and slow to rest. I lacked strength and spirit for a respectable cruise. It was time to go home; and so on a bright August morning I paddled down to the Forge House, hung the canoe up in Barrett's boathouse, and the cruise of the *Nipper* was ended, for one season at least.

Perhaps at some time in the near future, I will have a word to say regarding the cost, healthfulness, and pleasure of a trip to the North Woods, as compared to a our among the mountains of the Upper Susquehanna.

Forest and Stream, June 28, 1883

CRUISE
OF THE
SAIRY
GAMP

Oh, the beauties and delights of rural surroundings. The cheerful awakening from sound, healthful slumber. For instance, the time is about 4 a.m., or a little before. Dick, the game-cock, having gone to roost at sundown, suddenly awakens to a sense of his responsibility as boss of the entire premises and sends out a clarion note that may be heard one mile awal. Nine female geese and one old gander at once respond, with outstretched necks and voices shrill and deep. Three guinea hens, with their Brigham, take up the cry. The old peacock gets on his wings, sails up to the peak of the barn, and lets go to the bottom of his lungs. A flock of ducks starts up suddenly and waddles off to the creek with much noisy quacking. Four mild-eyed, deer-faced Alderney cows commence a musical bellowing from the paddock on the flat by the creek; four fawn-like calves answer with responsive bleatings from the calf-pasture above.

It is not yet 5 a.m., and the thrush, the robin, the song sparrow, the phoebe-bird, the catbird, the peewee, the chewink, the bluejay and the vireo are making the whole business very musical.

How about the awakening of a summer morning in New York? I am not so certain. I have tried both sides. I prefer the donkey engine to the guinea hen; the steam whistle to the peacock. The rattle and roar of the wakening city is hardly more disturbing to nerves than the racket of a farmyard. I know something better.

> I know a spot where plumy pines
> O'erhang the verdant banks of Otter,
> Where wood-ducks build among the vines,
> That bend above the crystal water.
> 'Tis there the bluejay makes her nest,
> In thickest shade of water beeches;
> The fish-hawk, statuesque in rest,
> Keeps guard o'er glassy pools and reaches.

Well, I am "going through the Wilderness." The *Sairy Gamp* meets me at Boonville the first week in July. The *Sairy* weighs ten and one half pounds. I noticed since I commenced writing about light canoes in *Forest and Stream*, several makers have discovered that a ten-pound canoe will carry a light canoeist and his duffle. Have they ever seen it done? Have they placed a few ten-pound canoes in the hands of skilled canoeists for lone, independent cruises in the North Woods and other glorious lake-dotted forests? Am I to meet one of them here and there, go into camp with him, divide the last ounce of provisions, and then paddle in company with him over the blessed clear waters, and over the inlets, outlets, etc.? I guess not. There is no ten, eleven or twelve-pound cedar canoe afloat this season with a live man in her.

I think a sixteen-pound canoe would be safer and more comfortable. All the same, she is bound to go through. Maybe she will do better than her maker thinks. Possibly he has builded better than he knew. There is a possibility that I may turn out to be an old gray-headed expert in light canoeing. Maybe I have been there. Perhaps I have paddled a *kyak,* the most ticklish boat that ever floated a man. And I may get drowned. I shall certainly take in some duckings.

Raquette Lake, July 27 (*F & S*, Aug. 9, 1883)

Thus far the *Sairy Gamp* has brought me in safety, and without wetting me once. The *Sairy,* I may remark, is a Rushton canoe, weighing just ten and one-half pounds.

And it is not that I may boast of cruising the lightest canoe ever built of cedar, that I paddle such an eggshell by river and lake through the Northern Wilderness. Not for the cheap notoriety that leads a man to tempt the ocean in a dory. But I have been testing light canoes for years, and my experiences may be of some value to the future canoeist who contemplates a lone cruise with the double blade.

We, the "outers," who go to the blessed woods for rest and recreation, are prone to handicap our pleasures in the matter of overweight; guns, rods, duffle, boats, etc. We take a deal of stuff to the woods, only to wish we had left it at home, and end our trips by leaving dead loads of impedimenta in deserted camps.

I should be glad to see this amended. I hope at no distant day to meet independent canoeists, with canoes weighing twenty pounds or less, at every turn in the wilderness, and with no more duffle than is absolutely necessary.

I met the *Sairy* at Boonville; also my old friend, Si Holliday, who contracted to land her at Moose River without a scratch; and he did it, though he came within an ace of capsizing. At Moose River I stayed several days, fishing for brook trout, testing and practicing canoe and paddle, likewise trying to brace up weak muscle, which sadly needed it.

I found the canoe much stauncher and steadier than I had been led to expect. Her maker had warned me that he would not warrant her for an hour. "She may go to pieces like an eggshell," he said. He had tested her with his own weight (110 pounds), and she closed in at gunwales an inch or more. He advised bracing her, and he thought with me and my duffle aboard she would only be two or two and a half inches out of water at center. "He builded better than he knew." She does not close in perceptibly at gunwales, and she has full five inches rise above water when on a cruise, with her skipper and light cargo properly stowed.

The only part of the cruise to be dreaded was the thirteen and one half miles of muddy, rock trail between Moose River and the Forge House, called the "Brown's Tract Road." I dared not trust her on the buckboards, and I hardly felt like making such a carry at the start; but I did it. I started before 5 a.m. and made the first three miles bravely. Began to weaken a little. Got some breakfast and went on. At the "six-mile tree" felt beaten. Buckboard came along with party. Party got out to lift and admire canoe. Driver said if I would leave my knapsack at the tree he would fetch it in on his return. Left it gladly.

Went on and got caught in drenching thunder storm. Crept under canoe until it passed over. Road a muddy ditch. At the "eight-mile tree" caught another and harder storm. Kept sulkily on, too mad and demoralized to dodge under canoe. Arrived at "ten-mile tree" pretty much tired and stopped (4 p.m.) to get some tea and lunch. Felt it to be the hardest carry I had ever made, and wished I had gone in by Jones's camp and the Stillwater of Moose River, as I had always done on previous trips.

Just then along came Ned Ball, a muscular young guide, and though he had four hounds in charge, he volunteered to hoist the canoe on his head and carry it in. "It don't weigh more'n a stovepipe hat," he said.

The last three and one-half miles of road were much better, and at 8 p.m. I arrived at the Forge House wet, bruised, and looking like an ill-used tramp. Some dry woolens, much too large, with a bright fire in front of the hotel, a night's rest, and a good breakfast brought me around and "paradise, reached through purgatory," was attained. Paradise meaning Brown's Tract, and purgatory, the twenty-five and one-half miles of wretched road between Boonville and the Forge House. That is how the admirers of Brown's Tract put it.

And the *Sairy* was safe on the lakes at last, without check or scratch. I paddled her about the first four lakes of the chain. Practiced getting into and out of her in difficult places and best of all, caught all the speckled trout I wanted, sitting in her at the springholes. This mode of fishing I pronounce the culmination of piscatorial sport. With a one-pound trout on the hook it was not necessary to yield more than a yard or two of line at the start, and then play the fish to a standstill by the easy movement of the canoe, reeling up to about ten feet of line, leading the fish about as one pleased, and let him tow the canoe until he turned on his side utterly exhausted, and refusing to raise a pectoral in defense of his life. Then gaff him by sticking a thumb in his open mouth and taking him in.

I had a very fair amount of this kind of sport and came to have a deal of confidence in the *Sairy* as I learned her light but reliable ways. I visited the camps, picked up old acquaintances, was fed daily on trout, got up better muscle, and, best of all, gained health with every day's exercise and sport. I found new camps on all the lakes, while the old camps were enlarged or improved, and fishing, I am pleased to say, much better than when I was here two years ago. This may be owing to restocking the lakes and streams. At any rate, I have seen thrice as many trout during a little more than two weeks' stay in the woods as I saw in twice the time two years ago.

In spite of the exceptionally cold, wet summer, sportsmen and healthseekers are enjoying the woods most satisfactorily. With at least five out of every six who come to this region for health, the improvement is decided and speedy. I have personal knowledge of some cases that seem almost marvelous; but there is a case here and there, mostly asthmatic, with which the cool, damp air does not agree. I know of two such cases. But I have conversed with a score who have gained in health to an extent that exceeded their most sanguine expectations.

There is some complaint about the winged things that bite and sting. Black flies were bad early in the season, and mosquitoes, as well as punkies, were never hungrier or plentier. To the man who prepares himself for the North Woods by getting up a pelt like a cellar-grown potato sprout and then runs a clipper over his head to give the insects a fair chance, no doubt they are a constant torment; especially if he is too aesthetic to use his fly medicine copiously, or so cleanly as to wash it off every day.

As for myself—even on Brown's Inlet—they pass me by as if I were a hot griddle. On starting in I established a good, substantial glaze, which I am not fool enough to destroy by any weak leaning to soap and towels.

I once published the recipe for insects in *Forest and Stream,* but will close by giving it once more. It is as follows: three oz. pure tar, two oz. castor oil, one oz. oil pennyroyal. Simmer together thoroughly, apply copiously, and don't fool with soap and water till you are out of the woods.

Forest and Stream, Aug. 16, 1883

Having loafed about Moose River for a week, and spent another week loitering, fishing, and paddling about the Fulton Chain, it struck me that, if the little canoe was to carry me on a cruise to the other side, it was time she was about it. I had several excuses for such utter laziness. I said the weather was too stormy, too "catching" for a start through the woods in a boat where a man can carry no change of clothes save an extra blue shirt and a pair of socks.

Moreover, I had met with an accident on the Brown's Tract Road that made my port deadlight look as though I had been in a "fight mit table legs" at "Hans Breitman's Barty"; looking like a tramp with a black eye, I disliked to introduce the *Sairy* among strangers. Again, there was good fishing, good fare, and plenty of deer about the Fulton Chain. True, we might not shoot the deer just yet. But it looked wholesome and woodsy to see them come down in broad daylight and feed fearlessly within sixty rods of the hotel, while the ladies waved their handkerchiefs, and the party chatted in tones that must have been very audible to sharp, cervine ears. I shall not soon forget one brave old fellow who came down to the water's edge, raised his antlered front boldly, calmly surveyed the party at the hotel, and then resumed his feed among the lilies.

"The old rascal knows it's close time," remarked a guide. "He won't be quite so tame after the first of August."

But there came a bright, clear afternoon, with good promise of one clear day, and the next morning the *Sairy* was making good time up the inlet of Fourth Lake.

The little Fifth, containing only nine acres, but good for floating and frogging, was run over in a few minutes; and then came the first carry, only three-quarters of a mile, but a muddy landing, and, like all carries, including "taking out" and "tieing in."

The Sixth Lake is made a desolation by the dam at its foot. The large, desolate rock on the left as you paddle up looks the more dreary for the dead timber at its base, and the inlet that leads to Seventh is a dismal swamp.

The trees around the once bright shores of the Seventh were dying when I was there two years ago. They are dead enough now. But the open camp, fifty rods to the left, is still there, and I turned to it for rest and a lunch. And as my newly-made fire sent up its smoke, there came a succession of rifle shots from the opposite side of the lake, a mile away, as of those who go through the wilderness wasting cartridges with poor aim and no object.

Then a boat pulled out and came swiftly to my camp. I had met the two occupants before. They reported that "Slim Jim" (James P. Fifield) was on the opposite side with a bark camp and a "party." He would like to see me. Now, Jim had been very friendly to me on previous visits to the woods, and I could not go by. So I paddled over for a hand-shake and an hour's chat. The time passed too quickly; and by the time I got back, made some tea and got packed up, it was nearly 3 p.m.

There were two carries (one of a mile, the other a mile and a half) with nine miles of water between me and my destination on the Raquette, and it was time to move. Over the desolate Seventh, up the drowned-out inlet, tie in, and over the carry to the Eighth and last lake of the chain. Here is a lake to admire and camp. No dam has backed up the water here. The bright green shores are as nature made them. Dunning's lone island is still a sylvan, restful emerald set in peaceful waters; and, by the way, Dunning was not at home, and as I couldn't burgle into his camp I thought it as well to play the paddle, for there is no landing on Brown's Tract Inlet, and if, at the mouth, it should happen to get backed in by rough water on Raquette, it would be most unpleasant.

So I hurried over the lake, took a short rest by the spring on the right, tied in, and went for the inlet on time. In thirty minutes I was afloat, and in an hour and ten minutes more was at the mouth. Luckily there was little wind—just the rolling swell a canoeist loves—and I turned down the shore of South Bay for a leisurely two-mile pull to the new camp of Joe Whitney, longtime guide, trapper and hunter, though being crippled in his best arm.

When he saw the tiny canoe and found I was cruising through the wilderness alone, I think his old hunter's heart went out to me. He welcomed me like a brother and got me up a supper consisting mainly of crisp trout, with fresh bread and butter, and powerful tea. If there was anything more I did not need it, and have forgotten. There is a sort of freemasonry among woodsmen that only woodsmen know. Joe and I had heard something of each other—not much; it took us about five minutes to get acquainted. In two hours we were thick as thieves.

While he was caring for the supper duffle, I was building a rousing fire before the camp. Both understood by instinct that no lamps or indoor arrangements were in order; and we squatted around the fire until "deep on the night," swapping forest yarns and hunting adventures. Then Joe showed me a bed, springy, fresh and clean, whereon I slept sweetly, but awoke in time to take in a glorious sunrise on scenery that I shall not disgrace by attempting to describe. It was all the more welcome in that sunrises during the summer of 1883 have been mostly inferential.

I half felt that on such a morning I ought to strike out and make Long Lake before night. But the day and the scenery were so delightful, the camp was so quiet, so restful, and the air so dry, so redolent of balsam and pine, that I let the hours go by, and the day wane in utter rest and indolence. What though? May there not come one glorious day in the weary year when we may cast aside every grief and every separate care and invite the soul to a day of rest? And in the future, when the days of trouble come, as they will come, I shall remember that grand day of rest, and the abundance of trout and bass wherewith I was comforted.

A finer, brighter morning never dawned on the clear waters of Raquette Lake than the one on which I paddled out from the fragrant, balsam-breathing camp of honest Joe Whitney for a new-made private camp on a point near Ed Bennett's, where I laid off while an enthusiastic young photographer took the *Sairy* in different positions, with and without her crew.

Then, by invitation, I went over the camp as amateur inspector, and although I have inspected dozens of these woodland residences called camps—all of them inviting and redolent of balsam and pine—I have seen none in more perfect sylvan taste than Camp Dick. I never feel the lack of wealth so sadly as when visiting these private camps, where, with a camp costing several thousand dollars, all in the way of food and drink that one can ask, two or three guides at $3 each per day, good fishing and hunting, the best of air and sweet sleep by night, one may dream away the hot summer solstice without ache, pain or care.

"And it is not so very costly," said one of the fortunate ones, "not so expensive as the watering places. I bring my family here during the summer months and get out of it for about $3,000 the season." Yes, it is cheap—for a millionaire. But it would break some of us to run such a camp for a single week. Fortunately, the woods are free, and we can make our own camps.

I stopped at Ed Bennett's Under the Hemlocks and then paddled slowly over to the Raquette House, kept by Ike Kenwell, and well kept, too. The selection of this hotel site was judicious. It stands—the hotel—on a dry breezy point of land jutting out into the lake, and it is always cool in the hottest weather. The house is well furnished, the table good, and the open bark camp with its fragrant bed of browse and rousing fire in front at night is a delightful woodland affair that should always be a part of the wilderness hotel. The best bass fishing on the lake is in easy reach of the landing.

Just at night I went down to the Forked Lake landing and carried over to the Forked Lake House, where I had a good supper, and watched a couple of guides organize their boat and jack for floating, though the close season had not expired. They were out nearly all night, and if they got a deer they kept their own. On the next night, however, a couple of guides went out and got a yearling buck. "It was so near the open season," they said, "what odds did it make if the deer were killed on Monday instead of Wednesday? The boarders were wild for venison." I think they were not so far wrong.

The second morning was clear (the previous day had been stormy) and I pulled out for the foot of Forked Lake, where I found Bill Cross, engaged as of old in hauling boats across the mile and a half carry. He took my knapsack over the carry out of good nature, and I paddled leisurely down the river, and down Long Lake to the newly-made Grove House, kept by Dave Helms [see plate XX]. Dave is a well-known Long Lake guide, who, having got a little ahead, and well knowing the requirements of tourists and sportsmen, concluded to give up guiding and take the chances of keeping a woodland resort. And he does more than well. "And it will be colder than it is now if I get left on venison after the first of August," says Dave.

It is at these less pretentious houses where the landlords have mostly been guides that I find the best fare and most sport when I care to fish or hunt.

And I write this gossipy letter because I am laying off

for the subsidence of a strong N. W. wind and rain. For I am not going to cruise the longest lake in the wilderness with wind and rain abeam. The *Sairy* is too light of tonnage for much extra clothing. A spare blue shirt and a pair of socks for change are all the clothing that goes on her manifest.

Forest and Stream, Aug. 23, 1883

Just for one day the rain held up, and a brighter morning never dawned on Raquette Lake than the one on which I paddled out for a cruise across the lake. The water was like a mirror, the air was perfect. It was a day to be marked with a white pebble. I had several invitations to visit private camps, and I availed myself of them pretty largely. I found several of these camps most delightful; gotten up with the utmost care and in excellent sylvan taste. I had occasion to note that venison and trout were always forthcoming, in moderation, though the close season for deer was not quite over.

But a game constable whom I interviewed rather had the idea to my notion. He said, "I ain't here to spoil sport, but to save the deer and help sportsmen to a good time. If I catch a man slaughterin' or crustin', I'll make it red-hot for him. But if I meet one of the boys with a party who has been two or three days on the side lakes and ponds floatin', I ain't goin' through their pack-baskets." Few sportsmen kill deer enough to hurt the increase of deer. Most of the breech-loaders brought into the wilderness never perforate anything more sensitive than an empty tin can. But, if there were no deer, and no fishing, how many would come to the Northern Wilderness?

And on the glorious day above mentioned, I had a taste of genuine, healthy, woodland pleasure. For once it did not rain, and I was dry—no small item for a man who runs too light for even a change of clothes, beyond a blue woolen shirt and a pair of yarn socks.

I left the Raquette for Forked Lake, and the demon of storms resumed his sway once more. I was detained by bad weather again at Fletcher's, the only compensation being a full supply of venison and the best of black bass. The latter have become more abundant, both in Forked and Raquette lakes, and the pure, cold water assures the quality.

On the first morning when it did not rain, I got an early start down the lake and the Raquette River for Long Lake, *via* the rapids and Buttermilk Falls—since Adirondack Murray's book, called Phantom Falls. And, as on a previous occasion, I spent an hour watching the dashing, foaming water and footing up the utter impossibility of any man or boat ever tumbling over those ragged boulders and coming out anything but corpse and kindling wood.

I made the river and the three carries, sighting one deer and chasing a flock of ducks for a mile. The deer walked leisurely off. The ducks kept just ahead for awhile, and finally huddled into a little cove and let me pass them within thirty yards. I carry no breech-loader through the woods. My only weapon is a jackknife, and that not loaded. Deer and ducks were safe from me.

A mile below the last carry I turned in to land at the new camp of Dave Helms, erst guide, and now landlord of a most pleasant camp or hotel (all the moderate sized hotels are camps here). I found his site beauti-

fully chosen, on a piney, breezy, sandy point, high, dry
and healthy, his charges very moderate, and, no slight
item, good hunting and fishing in easy reach. Parties
came across the woods from Blue Mountain, complain-
ing that charges were high, no fishing or hunting; nothing to do but loaf around the stylish hotels or row on
Blue Mountain Lake. I recommended them to try a
week or two with Dave.

When a morning came that promised well, I once more
paddled out, my destination being the Platt camp, three
miles from the foot of Long Lake. This time I had a
pleasant breeze and no rain, the wind being dead aft, a
most desirable thing with a double-blade. I found Sen-
ator Platt in camp, and a pleasant visit, fish, venison with
open bark camp and huge log fire in front go far to com-
pensate for the almost daily soakings I have caught since
leaving the Forge House.

I ought to mention that Helms' camp is only twenty-
five rods from the house of John Plumley, "Honest
John," Murray's guide for several seasons.

It goes without saying that I made his acquaintance,
and asked him some leading questions concerning his
work as Murray's guide. He said, "Murray was a good
woodsman. He came in with his wife, and guided himself sometimes. He could take his boat over the carries
as well as I could. The big trout? Oh, yes. He caught a
good many large trout. The one he caught in his 'Nameless Creek' was not the largest I saw him take. He was
a capital hand with the flyrod. His 'Nameless Creek"
was the inlet of Shallow Lake. It was just boiling with
jumping trout that evening. As to his shooting Buttermilk Falls, any fool who takes one look at the falls knows

better. But we both did run the rapids, both the upper and lower. It is a little risky, but is often done. Sometimes a man leaves all but his seats and oars, but I never broke up a boat there. I don't think Murray meant to say that he ever ran the falls. Yes, I am on the guide list yet. Have got a party as soon as I can get my hay in."

And so much for honest John Plumley, one of the experienced guides who can paddle you up to a deer by night, or put you on to a springhole where big trout abound, with the best.

On leaving the Platt camp my good luck on weather deserted me. It was ten and a half miles to go by lake, river and carry to Mother Johnson's. The last three miles were made in a soaking rain that left me without a dry thread. The next morning, being once more dried out, I swung out in the little *Sairy* for a seven-mile paddle down the Raquette and up Stony Creek Ponds to the Hiawatha House (Dukett's). For once I had dry weather and a pleasant trip, though the wind was high. After dinner I carried over to Corey's (three-quarters of a mile) [see plate XXI] and spent the afternoon examining some models of Adirondack boats, interviewing guides, boat builders, etc., and looking over the Upper Saranac, which looked altogether too rough for the *Sairy*. So I decided for once to relieve tired muscles by a ten-mile ride on the little steamer that navigates the lake.

I had already paddled more than the distance from side to side of the wilderness, and if it looked like dodging to avoid water on which the canoe could not live, so be it.

Paul Smith's, Adirondacks.

Forest and Stream, Sept. 13, 1883

The little steamer that plies on the Upper Saranac makes the different landings in a zig-zag manner that knocks the compass points endwise. Only by staying where you can watch every turn of the prow can you retain a definite notion of north and south. And that is how it happened that, being unobservant of turns, I found the sun setting in the east—a vexatious thing to a woodsman. Missing one of the turns of the boat, I was turned myself. I straightened myself out by shutting both eyes and letting a muscular guide whirl me around half a dozen times promiscuously, then setting the compass without looking at the sun; then, being right on the cardinal points, I took a general average of the landscape. This brought me right.

Bartlett's Landing is a ten minutes' easy walk from the hotel [see plate XXII]. The house was well filled with boarders, and when the captain of the steamer got a little enthusiastic in describing the little canoe, nearly the entire force of the house, eager for any novelty, turned out to take a look at her. I think that not less than fifty people had a turn at lifting her. Then they wanted to see her go. So I took off boots and coat, got in, and paddled out into the lake, where there was a swell that made her dance like a cork. Then down the lake, with a whole sail breeze after us, bright weather, and the principal mountain peaks in sight all the way. Very pleasant, but it came to an end.

A night at the Prospect House, and a most exasperating draw across a muddy carry of four miles, where I hung onto the canoe until my arms were numb, and

I launched on Big Clear Pond, only to get caught in an ugly squall and drenching rain once more. I paddled up to honest Joe Baker's camp, wet to the skin, and got a privilege by the cook stove, which I held until bed time.

The next day brought a steady, persistent, all-day rain; tiresome to a degree. I relieved the tedium by playing the mouth organ for Joe's children, talking to anybody who would listen, and baking my mouth with five-cent cigars. Monday, the 6th, was clear and cold. I hired Joe to take myself and canoe across the two-mile carry on a one-horse wagon, and found it the roughest, muddiest carry I had yet encountered.

Crossed the Upper St. Regis Lake to Spitfire Pond, where, for the first time, I was driven ashore by a sharp sea and a flawy wind that bade fair to catch under the canoe and capsize her. I crept through the brush along shore until I reached the outlet, paddled to the Lower St. Regis, where I was again beaten off and landed on Captain Peter's Rock in front of the hotel, where, less than half a mile off, I could see conviviality and comfort and pleasant verandas where couples were promenading and children playing about the grounds of Paul Smith's noted woodland resort.

And I was hungry and likewise thirsty. If there be creature comforts anywhere in the woods, they may be found at Paul Smith's. But there was a white-crested, topping sea between me and the comforts aforesaid. Even the stiffest guide-boats shunned the rough sea from Peter's Rock to the outlet, and kept along the smoother windward shore. So I amused myself by putting a board shanty which stands on the rocky point in order, picking blueberries, cutting wild grass and making believe I was going to camp all night within one hundred and fifty rods of a first-class hotel.

It was, on the whole, very enjoyable. The weather, barring the heavy wind, was dry and bright. I sat on the warm, mossy rock and recalled all the wild forest yarns I had heard of Cap'n Peter. I half hoped that the wind would rise to a gale and hold me there all night. Once I got up my sand, "tied in" and made a straight wake for the hotel. Ten rods out a black flaw caught the *Sairy* at the garboard streak and nearly lifted her over. I watched for a "smooth," turned her, and struck out again for Cap'n Peter's Rock.

Late in the afternoon, when the wind had subsided somewhat, a strong boat with two guides in her came over purposely to give me a lift "across the stormy water." At first I demurred. I would paddle over when the wind fell a little. I could "make the riffle," etc. But they said there were parties at the hotel who were anxious to see the little canoe and the little old woodsman who had paddled and carried her over 118 miles. So I weakened and allowed myself to be taken in tow.

Luckily, Paul Smith [see plate XXIII] happened to know me—by reputation—and he met me cordially. Grand old woodsman he is. Once a guide, and a good one. Now, the most successful landlord in the Northern Wilderness. Not so old as one who has followed the writers of the North Woods would infer. Only fifty-six, and well preserved. I am glad to have met him. More than glad to have crossed from side to side of this region without its parallel on the globed earth.

On the 12th of this month, Verplanck Colvin meets a commission at Blue Mountain to report on the expediency of preserving this grand region as a State park. May their counsels be guided by good common sense and humanitarian principles, and no politics, log-rolling, or hippodroming allowed the slightest consideration.

Paul Smith's, August, 1883.

Little Tupper Lake, Aug. 12 (*F & S*, Sept. 13, 1883)

I date from Little Tupper Lake, and a finer lake it would be hard to find. No desolate lines of drowned out lands here. All as it came from the hands of nature. Have been out this morning deer hunting, so to speak. Laid off for four mortal hours waiting for a deer to attempt the crossing of Dukett's Bay. No deer came. But there came a loon, and he settled within ten rods of the canoe, raised himself on hind legs (they are very hind, and he has no others), turned his white, clean breast to me and gave me his best weird, strange song. Clearer than a clarion, sweeter than a flute, loud enough to be heard for miles.

Never, as my soul lives, will I draw a bead on a loon. He is the very spirit of the wildwoods. Fisherman he may be. He catches his daily food after his nature. He is no trout crank. He does not catch trout at fifty cents per pound for the hotels. Don't, please don't, emulate Adirondack Murray and waste two dozen cartridges in the attempt to demolish a loon.

Every sportsman who enters the office of Paul Smith's hotel will notice the neat, well-mounted buck's head at the right, as one goes in. The head and horns are in nowise remarkable. The horns are only four points to the side. I have saved a score of better heads myself. But the head is flanked on either side by an immense speckled trout. Paul Smith gave me this account of them. He said: "Mr. Hotchkiss and his partner, of New Haven, went out fishing on Big Clear Pond. Mr. Hotchkiss hooked the biggest trout, and saved him. They had a lot more, weighing from one to three pounds. I said, what are you going to do with these big trout? Give them to me and I will have them mounted. They did. I sent them to Bell, of New York, and he sent them back, as you see, with a bill for $43. I don't regret it. I have been offered $100 for them."

The success of the St. Regis is as nothing to me. But, the grand old woodsman. The man who fell in love with the little canoe; who gave me points on the return trip; who talked with gusto of his guiding days, when he guided Charles Hallock and many other notables of the woodland fraternity; well, I am not likely to soon forget him.

I will pause to remark that, of the two big trout, the one on the left, facing the deer's head, weighed by scale five and one-quarter pounds. The one at the right four and one-half pounds. And I have been after a big trout for fifty years, and the biggest trout I ever caught weighed less than two pounds! Well, I am no trout liar.

Paul Smith's woodland resort is rather a high-toned institution—a sort of sylvan Long Branch; a forest Newport. Coaches arrive every day quite after the style of fifty years ago. Full inside, six on top; guard playing a loony tune on a preposterously long tin horn. Billiards, tenpins, finely-kept playgrounds, good drives, good livery, and, what I did not expect, good trouting and deer hunting within easy reach of the hotel. It was on the eve of August 8. I had packed my slender duffle, had "tied in," and was promising myself an early daylight start on the following morning.

The evening was fine, the walks and piazzas were thronged, a dozen guides were gathered in front of the hotel talking dog, deer, trout, parties, etc., after the manner of guides in the North Woods. And there came from the outlet a swift, double-ended blue boat with only a guide in her, and the guide was giving her an ash breeze for all she was worth.

He ran his boat high and dry on the clean sandy beach, came quickly up to the knot of guides, and said curtly, "Boys, Joe Newell's drowned."

"Where? When? How?" were the hurried questions.

"In Follensby, Jr. Two hours ago; fell out of his boat somehow and tangled up in the lily-pads."

There was silence and soberness among the guides. Finally one remarked, "Somebody ought to tell his wife."

"Jim, you go up and tell her."

"I—I can't. I've got to wash my boat and take my party up the lake. Why don't you go?"

"Wouldn't do it for a hundred dollars. Let the clerk send a boy."

Then the guides arranged for an early start over to Follensby Pond to grapple for the body; and a gloom seemed to settle on the pleasant surroundings as the news spread. And the question most often heard was "Has anyone told his wife?" I don't think I should like to be the one to carry her the news.

On the morning of the 9th at 4:30 a.m. I quietly stepped into the little canoe for the return trip by a somewhat different route. No one was astir about the hotel save the night watchman, who came down to the landing to see me off. Through the Lower St. Regis, Spitfire Pond, the Upper St. Regis, the two-mile carry, and I reached Joe Baker's in time for breakfast. Then a delightful trip of two miles across Big Clear brought me to Sweeney's; a half-mile carry to Little Clear Pond, with its bright waters and beautiful shores.

If I wanted to go into camp for a week or two for fishing and hunting, I have no ground I would prefer to the pleasant, lonely banks of Little Clear Pond. It is well stocked with both lake and brook trout. And a young Sweeney who helped me on the carry said, "Lake trout have been taken here weighing twenty-five pounds. Then, the fish commission had a hatchery just back of that point, and they turned thousands of speckled and lake trout into the pond—but few come here to fish—and there ain't a better stocked lake in the woods. Speckled trout don't do so well here, the paint bothers 'em."

"The paint?"

"Yes, ochre paint. You can catch a tin can full in a few minutes. Good paint, too. It keeps brook trout away from the spring holes, and in the deep water the lakers gobble them. Deer are plenty. I saw a big buck in the pond last evening, but he kept so near the shore I couldn't cut him off."

Over the two and a half mile carry to the Prospect House, across the Saranac to the Sweeney Carry, and down the carry to the desolate, drowned-out shores of the once beautiful Raquette River [a dam built in 1870 at Piercefield Falls flooded the low-lying land along the Raquette for thirty miles upriver]. And get down and out of the Raquette in the quickest possible time. A sluggish, sullen stream, with miles on miles of dead timber and unnatural marsh, is not the stream to linger on; and you will be glad, as I was, that there is a little steamer to speed you out of it and land you at the head of Big Tupper in time for supper.

Half a mile above the hotel you may see a foaming sheet of water tumbling into the lake over brown, wholesome-looking boulders. This is Boy Falls [Bog Falls], and a carry of a few rods sets the canoe afloat above and beyond dead shore lines. The cruise up Boy Stream [Bog River] is bright and pleasant. The carries are a little rough and muddy, but the run across Round Pond and up the channel into Little Tupper makes amends while the hunter-like welcome to be met at the Grove House inclines one to lay off for a few days and take a little hunting, as it were.

For Pliny Robins is hunter and guide, as well as landlord, and has even now started up the lake with his rifle and two eager hounds in the boat. A guide with two more hounds is just launching his boat, and it looks a good deal like a hunt. I notice a quarter of venison still left in the store-room. I have not eaten a meal since I came here without trout or venison, one or both. Such fare is always to be had at Little Tupper. Both deer and trout are becoming more plentiful yearly, partly through better protection for the one and judicious restocking for the other.

The number of beautiful lakes and ponds in this wonderful region, no man knows, and Little Tupper is among the finest. Gamy as the gamiest, clear as the clearest, and seldom rough. Where there are so many delightful sheets of water, each with its own peculiar beauties, it is idle to claim any one as *par excellence* the finest.

The *Sairy* has been fairly paddled up to date. I am called on about every day to take her out and show her paces for the benefit of the curious or skeptical. I mostly comply. I am pleased to show people how light a boat will carry a man safely and comfortably. She is to go back by the Slim Pond route, and Long Lake, Forked, Raquette, etc., to my favorite stamping ground, the waters of the Moose.

Forest and Stream, Sept. 20, 1883

One of the puzzles that will be apt to fog the lone canoeist is the repetition of names as applied to ponds, lakes and streams. For instance, take Stoddard's map. You will find nine "Clear Ponds," seven "Mud Ponds," six "Long Ponds," six "Wolf Ponds," four "Rock Ponds," several "Round Ponds," etc., etc. And you will find these names repeated in many localities where no ponds or lakes are indicated on the map. To the man who has studied the Wilderness, these repetitions are of little account. But I was surprised when old guides of twenty-five years' standing cooly disputed me on this point and were hardly convinced by reference to the map. But this was to be expected.

The Forge House guide is bound to know the waters of the Moose River, north and south branches, with the Fulton Chain, side lakes, spring holes, and all places where trout do most abound or deer are successfully floated. He has camps thereon and takes his parties thereunto. So of the Beaver guide, the Saranac guide, Long Lake, etc., etc. But none of them are guides for the whole Wilderness, and never can be.

Life is not long enough to learn this mystic region in

its entirety. A few of the oldest have a knowledge of this region that is wonderful, and only to be acquired by a life devoted to guiding. Among them are such men as Mitchell Sabattis, Sam Dunakin, Alvah Dunning, Lon Wood, Paul Jones, John Brinkerhoff and Pliny Robins. Most of these are waxing old. Alvah Dunning is sixty-eight. Many of the best guides are on the wrong side of fifty, and the younger guides can not fill their places, though willing and strong.

Sportsmen understand this but too well. Recently, while young guides at Blue Mountain were waiting in vain for parties, Sabattis had thirty applications in one day from parties who knew the famous old Indian guide by reputation; and a dozen guides, just as good, were waiting for employment. It is right that the older guides have first choice of parties. They have knowledge of spring holes where large trout may be taken by the tyro. They know unmapped, nameless lakes where any greenhorn can get a shot at a deer within twenty yards. They are all good cooks. It is their religion to take care of their parties. Once you employ a guide he is yours. His platform is simple—to care for his party as a mother cares for her child; not to wet you, and to die sooner than leave you on a long, dismal carry. I have known a guide to pack a sick man over three hard carries by the light of a lantern; then go back and double-trip the carries for his fool duffle of rods, guns, etc., etc., with no extra charge.

N.B.—When you take a guide, tie to him.

The man who finds himself at the camp of Pliny Robins, with an intention of going out to the westward, will do well to study the routes by which he can "make the riffle." Firstly, there is the route by Smith and Albany lakes [now Nehasane Lake and Lake Lila], Charley Pond, the stiff carry over to Twitchell Lake, over to Big Moose, down the North Branch [of the Moose River], through the North Branch lakes, over the carry to Fourth Lake. Fourteen miles of carries. Not so very interesting, and pretty hard, as all agreed. Then, there was the route by Rock and Bottle ponds. This promised better. There was good fishing. The scenery was very fine. The route would bring me to the head of Little Forked Lake, within six miles of Forked Lake Landing, which is within twelve miles of Raquette Lake.

I had nearly made up my mind to take this route, but Pliny Robins said, "Have you ever thought of the Slim Ponds route? Strikes me as the most interesting route, and I have traveled them all. Suppose you go over to Big Slim tomorrow, and come back. If you don't like it take Rock and Bottle Pond route." I did. When I was well fed on trout and venison, and the weather for once was too fine for description, I paddled across Little Tupper Lake, left the big leaning pine on the left, rounded the sharp point, paddled up to the head of the bay and found the landing easily.

There I hung up coat and boots, deciding to go through in stocking feet, for my feet are tough and perfect; I have no corns or bunions. I made the carry easily, "tied out," and was making for the easily-seen landing, sixty rods away, when an innocent bear paddled out from an island forty rods to the right and headed for a barren hill, half a mile distant. In an instant I froze down solid. Not a motion. I did not want to kill him or save him. But I thought to get up a little racket in the way of fun.

He was too sharp. He had probably seen the canoe. He rounded the point of the island, and although I gave him my best spruce breeze, I saw him no more. He might as well have kept on his course. I had nothing with which to hurt him more dangerous than a light pine paddle.

Then I took the carry from Stony Pond to Big Slim, going for a hundred rods on an easy path, then turning sharp to the right and taking the path down to a shaking bog, to the narrow, muddy ditch, which they call on the eastern side a "slang."

This "slang" was a mile long and so narrow that I brought in the paddle, laid it alongside, and made my way by pulling the canoe along by the weeds and water shrub on either side. It was a tedious job, but when I came out into the clear, bright waters and entire solitude of Big Slim Pond, I was well rewarded.

They have a way on the eastern side of calling a lake a pond. Big Slim Pond is a beautiful lake; narrow, long and lonely. One may here catch all the trout any reasonable sportsman may desire, and all of good size. Deer may be floated successfully on either Big or Little Slim. Half way down Big Slim there is a point jutting out to the right on which there is a pine bark camp, and just at this point one may catch fine trout at the mouth of the cold spring brook which comes brattling down by the camp. I noted all this for future reference and then made my way back to Pliny Robins' hotel.

The next day was fair, and as is my way, I paddled out at 5 a.m. I take the early day in canoeing when the winds are low. I lay my course the day before. If a dense fog covers the waters, as it often does, I lay the compass on the keelson before me and steer by the points. Men and women have deceived me often, the compass never. And so across Little Tupper by Stony Pond, Big Slim, Little Slim, Mud Pond, the three-mile carry, across Clear Pond [now Lake Eaton], the one-mile carry to Long Lake, and three miles up the lake I came again to the camp of honest Dave Helms. Rather glad to get there, I may say. I had camped overnight on Big Slim and caught—just one trout. He was fourteen inches long. I reeled up and quit at once. I wanted no more. Was I fishing for creels, counts or hotels? Rather not, I should remark. I take what I need, no more; I do not fish for hotels.

It was on the 15th of August that I reached the camp of Dave Helms. The law on hounding deer "runs out" on that day. There is a gentleman on an island in Raquette Lake — (or was), Mr. Charles Durant, of Adirondeck Railroad notoriety. This gentleman has a camp on Raquette Lake that looks like a Swiss villa. Having no excuse for obtruding myself upon him, I did not land at his camp; but I "laid off" and took stock of the camp as I passed up the lake; and if, as was said, the camp cost $15,000, I think it was reasonable, and cheap—for the man who could afford it.

Now, Mr. Durant had organized a hunt of feudal proportions, to come off on the 16th of August. Just the day I was going up from Long Lake to Raquette. I had, and have, a theory that I can gaff the largest deer in a light canoe and handle him as easily as I can a large trout. And so, on the morning of the 16th, with line and gaff in readiness, I paddled slowly up the head of Long Lake listening for hounds, but hearing none.

Going up the Raquette River and over the three carries, I rather made time. But once on Forked Lake I took it easy and looked for deer. I saw several blue boats along shore with guides and sportsmen ready to strike out and "cut off" the hapless deer that might take water. But I saw no deer, though I twice heard hounds in full cry. Resting, laying off, and slowly working my way to the Forked Lake House, I laid up the canoe a little before sundown and awaited reports. The reports began to come in about dark and continued until midnight. There had been thirty-six sportsmen in the hunt, with nineteen guides and thirty hounds, more or less. The results were, one fine buck and a small yearling. Eleven guides, who could find no room to spread their blankets at Durant's camp, rowed down to the Forked Lake House for quarters, and they rather made it lively. And there was high jinks at the Durant camp until "the wee short hour ayont the twal."

Gossip said that the hunt cost the originator of it $1,000. If so, he probably does not regret it. He might as easily have invested it on a single hand of draw-poker; with not a tithe of the sport.

Crossing Raquette Lake once more, I found Ed Bennett's place, "Under the Hemlocks," well stocked with guides, tourists, sportsmen and summer boarders all eager for any little excitement or novelty. Whence it happened, I suppose, that nearly all the force turned out to have a look at the little canoe. To lift her and exclaim on her lightness. To ask questions of the rough-looking little old duffer who had cruised her from side to side of the wilderness, and pretty well back again by a different route. Ed Bennett, who weighs 170 pounds, was bound to paddle the *Sairy*. He took his shoes off to get in.

"You promised to let me ride in her when you came back," said he.

"Not for twice her value. She might collapse like an eggshell. She is within forty-seven miles of the Moose River House. I know the route as well as any guide. If her frail siding should get broken now, I had as lief you broke my neck."

And I ported the double-blade, tied in strongly, and took the canoe up to the porch, "under the hemlocks."

At the landing I met honest Joe Whitney, who was *en route* for Blue Mountain Lake. Finding I was bound for his camp, he put me in care of Billy Cornell, a young guide who takes charge in his absence, saying, "Take good care of him, and keep him until I get back." And we walked over the point, crossed the beautiful bay, and were once more in the quiet, breezy camp of Joe Whitney.

Now, I was very glad of a chance for a visit and a talk with young Cornell. It happened that when I was at this same camp the last week in July, that Billy Cornell and another young man were off on a rather peculiar expedition, and Joe seemed very anxious about their return. He was looking for them the night of my arrival. They did not come until the next evening as the sun was sinking below the hills. They came up the bay wearily with oars and paddle, pretty well fagged out. They had two pack baskets, one containing about twenty pounds of large trout, the other holding the meat of a yearling buck. They had toted boat and baskets ten miles through tangled woods where there was no trail, and were too tired for much talk. They left me a couple of large trout, with some venison, and took the balance to Hathorn's camp, across the bay. It struck me as paying pretty dearly for the whistle, putting in three days of such work for a small deer and a basket of trout, and I said so.

"Well," said Joe, "the trout and venison were in order, seeing they were there and might as well take them in. But that wasn't what they went for. They went over to educate the deer."

I had a pretty close notion of what he meant, but was not going to ask questions, lest I give myself away. And, as I left at 5 a.m. the next morning, while the boys were sleeping like the dead, there was no chance for explanations.

But now that Billy Cornell had me in his care to feed, warm and look after; that the out-of-door fire was burning brightly; that he had paddled the *Sairy* about the bay as well as I could—his weight is just 141½ pounds— I thought it in order to ask, "By the way, how did you make it, educating the deer, and what was the object anyhow?"

Billy adjusted the fire, settled himself on his block, and thus explained: "You see, there are two ponds about ten miles from here that you won't find laid down on any map. And I doubt if you can find two ponds in the North Woods where more deer come to feed than right there. It is on the ground where my partner and I still-hunt in the fall and early winter, but is too far off for floating from this side. We can get good floating in a quarter of the distance.

"But on the other side there is a gang of half-breeds who make it a part of their religion to get in on the ponds on the last day of July and just go for slaughter. Last year they floated two nights and dragged off fifteen deer. This year we thought it might be well to cut them off.

So we packed boat and baskets ten miles through the woods and spent three days 'educating' deer. The ponds were swarming with them, and they were tamer than sheep. We would paddle up to the deer, and when within thirty or forty feet cut loose with four drams of powder and just a pinch of number thirteen shot, to sting him, so he wouldn't forget his lesson. We educated over a dozen the first night. The second night we took the other pond and gave free lessons to as many more. Not a deer of them will ever stand for a light again. Of course, the gang will come in and get a few deer this season, but they won't make slaughter-yards of the ponds as they did last year.

"We saved one little yearling buck. What moral difference was there between killing him on the night of the 20th or the 31st of July? And the camps all need venison. We saved every pound of the meat, and it was more than it was worth to pack it out. Yes, the best speckled trout fishing, and the best floating is on ponds, lakes and streams not down on the maps."

"And there are many of these?"

"Scores of them. Perhaps hundreds. I could take you, if you didn't mind some hard travel, to ponds where you could get half a dozen shots in a night, or catch all the trout you cared to pack out; and I don't set up for much of a guide."

It is true that along the traveled routes and where camps do most abound, deer have become wary and rather scarce, while trout are hard to get.

But, on the secluded lakes and ponds, far in the woods, away from frequented trails, deer and trout are most abundant.

Forest and Stream, Sept. 27, 1883

It was on the morning of August 17, at 5 a.m., that I paddled out from the Whitney camp, intending to make the Forge House by evening, distance twenty-seven miles, about four miles of it carries. I made the first eight miles before stopping for breakfast, but was caught in a shower and spent a couple of hours drying out.

I had stopped at Alvah Dunning's island on Eighth Lake and had depended on finding the key to his camp, as he told me where to look for it when I met him at Raquette Falls. But the key was gone and I was obliged to take an outside ticket. So I stole a couple of Alvah's shooks, improvised a dry platform, made a rousing fire on the lee side of his camp, also a pot of green tea—the kind that raises the hair — got out the old shelter tent for a bed, and, having had breakfast, was lounging and smoking, when, at the landing above, I saw a blue boat on a pair of blue legs walk down to the water and prepare to launch out. The legs had the balance of a guide-looking man above them, and the man shipped his oars in a businesslike way, headed for the island, and came speedily abreast of the camp.

I hailed, "Would he land?"

He resitated for a moment, backed water, and came to the landing. He proved to be Fred Loveland, landlord of the Boreas River House and one of the old-time guides. He was bound for the Forge House and was in no hurry. That was just my case. I proposed that we keep company, and he readily agreed. And so, by the bright green solitary shores of the Eighth Lake and over to the clean sandy landing, we went together, or rather he went ahead, and I followed after with such speed as a nine-foot canoe can make, with a head wind and a short snappy sea to beat with the broad double blade.

At the landing he tied in and asked me to hold up the stern while he crept under and adjusted the neck-yoke. "She is a brute of a boat," he added. "In twenty-five years of guiding I never carried but one such boat, and I never will carry another. Once I get her to the Forge, she may go to — the fool that built her. She weighs over one hundred pounds." And she did. Once we stopped to rest on the mile carry from Eighth down to Seventh, and, as I held up the prow again, his remarks were terse and sharp on a "boat that it took two men to shoulder."

Over the carry, down the dismal swamp (where I hung up all night two years ago), sometimes in the channel, sometimes out, and we began to feel the swell at the head of Seventh.

I had kept good pace with the guide down the crooked channel, but when I saw the white caps on the Seventh it struck me as rather an unsocial way of traveling, that one should go ahead with a long, sharp boat, and his companion come puffing along in the rear with a canoe little larger than a bread tray. Wherefore I fell in readily with the suggestion that the larger boat would "trim" better with two than one. Also, I may have had some doubts as to whether I could make the opposite shore at all.

Loveland adjusted his seats for two, I got into the stern and took hold of the bit of fish-line that serves the *Sairy* for a painter. She danced along like a cork, and we crossed the Seventh, with its dreary shore lines of dead timber, with scarcely a spoken word. Down the crooked outlet to the more dismal Sixth, with its accursed, ill-smelling dam. Here we "took out" for the last carry, from Sixth to Fifth. It is nearly three-quarters of a mile, but is rocky, tortuous and hilly. One thing can be said of the Fifth: it is still about as nature formed it. Also, it is good "frogging" ground, but only a pughole of nine acres.

Coming down the shallow outlet of the Fifth, the wisdom of having good company became very apparent—to me at least. There was a stiff topsail breeze blowing directly up the lake, and the white-crested waves at the head of the "Stormy Fourth" were piling up in a way that would have made it impossible for the *Sairy* to advance a rod in an hour. Not that I think the sea would have swamped her. But every wave would have lifted half her length out of water, the wind would have caught under her full bearings, also on the broad blades, and any progress would have been out of the question. Even the sturdy guide, with a well-handled pair of oars and a sharp, narrow boat, was sometimes brought to a standstill as we rounded an exposed point. Then there would come a lull and we would go ahead again. I think we were nearly two hours making the first three miles. There was no boat in sight but ours. Boats mostly avoid the head of the Fourth in a stiff wind.

When about half way down the lake we swung into a shallow bay to avoid the wind, and I saw, on the port bow, a neat, fresh-looking bark camp that appeared unoccupied. I called Loveland's attention to it, and, giving it one look, he turned and pulled straight for the landing without a word.

In ten minutes the boats were hauled up, I had a bright fire burning, and we had cleaned up an empty quart can for tea. He went to his boat and took out an oblong package which I noticed he had been very careful of, and the package developed into sandwiches, bread and cheese. My knapsack was capable of tea, sugar, butter and bacon, with tin-ware for cooking. There was a bed of fresh browse in the camp, and a fine spring nearby, with a rough table outside. Best of all, we were both wolf-hungry.

It was one of the impromptu, wholesome woodland dinners that are remembered through life, while the memory of more pretentious feasts have

> Gone, like the tenants that left without
> warning,
> Down the back entry of Time.

After dinner I suggested that we spend an hour or so smoking, lounging on the browse, and waiting for the wind to go down with the sun, and we did. There was no hurry. We had all the time there was, and the evening was almost certain to be fine, with a full moon. So we possessed our souls in patience and took turns smoking the only pipe we had between us.

"When the sun was very low, and wild winds bound within their Cell," we pulled over the remaining three miles of the now-placid Fourth, and I stopped at the foot to land at my old camp of three years ago, while Loveland rowed to Perrie's camp on Third Lake.

At Third Lake I found him and he urged me to take a seat in his boat to the Forge House, just for sociability; but I declined. I wanted to visit a little with old acquaintances, and also I had a fancy for taking in the lower three lakes by moonlight once more; for I had a presentiment that I was likely to go over them no more.

And when the moon rose, orange-red and large and full, I paddled, very quietly and a little sadly, over the Third, by the Eagle's Nest, across the Second, by the Stickney camp and over the First, and so down by the Indian Rock and down the channel until I made the lights of the Forge House. I landed at the boathouse, tied in, and at 8:30 o'clock the *Sairy* was resting by the maple tree where my canoes have so often found a safe resting place.

It had been a part of my programme to take in about two weeks of deer hunting on the branches of Moose River: wherefore I had left the old hair-triggered, nail-driving muzzle loader at the Forge House in charge of Charley Barrett.

For the first twenty-one days after leaving the Forge House for Paul Smith's I had nineteen rainy days, and all cold. This, with an accident that nearly paralyzed my right arm, made the cruise a slow affair. And it was not strange that I found my vacation of six weeks all gone. But I still lingered, stealing one more week. I had been just one month crossing the Wilderness and returning. It was as well so. I was not running on time. I stopped wherever and whenever I found objects of interest, or saw a chance to pick up useful knowledge of the noted North Woods. And now my time was up.

On the morning of August 24th I picked up the *Sairy* at 5 a.m. and started for the last day's cruise I shall probably make in her. By way of the Stillwater and Jones's camp, it is twenty miles to Moose River Tannery. And the route is not what it was three or even two years ago. It has fallen into disuse. The bridge at the old Arnold place has succumbed to time and now blocks the course, a dismal looking wreck. Huge trees have fallen across the stream and remain as they fell. And there are two ugly flood-jams that are so many terrors to a light canoe.

Cautiously and slowly I worked by all these, and then there was the Little Rapids. Two years ago I paddled the *Nipper* up these rapids, and never took out until I reached the Forge House landing. It was not so now. The gate at the foot of First Lake was raised, and a black and white torrent was rushing and roaring over the ragged sandstone boulders, looking a trifle dangerous for such a light craft. While I was hanging on at the head of the rapids, back-paddling and making up my mind whether to "shoot" them or carry around, fate decided the question. One of those colorless boulders caught the prow of the canoe, whirled her broadside on, and the next instant I *was* shooting the rapids, stern foremost. I think it was not five seconds until I was safely by the rocks and on the level, foamy current below. One bump and a jump on a rock that nearly threw me out, and I was calmly floating on deep, clear water.

Feeling a little faint I headed down stream and paddled leisurely to Jones's camp, thinking what a neat adventure it would have been had I been capsized, and the canoe gone down the river without me. Aye. But you see, she couldn't do it. The double-bladed paddle was tied to her ribbing with six feet of strong trolling line. I never let go of the paddle in an upset. I hang to the paddle. Paddle holds the canoe. See?

Jones's camp was deserted and desolate. A lively red

squirrel was the only live thing in sight or hearing. He had wired his way into Jones's horse barn and was living at free quarters. I was glad of it. I hope he will eat up ten bushels of chop-stuff and oats and call in his sisters, his cousins and his aunts. For Eri Jones flatly declined to "put me on" to the hiding place of his camp key. I stood about one chance in fifty of needing it. But if I did need it, I should need it badly. Luckily, it would have been of no use.

I took a half-hour's rest, nibbled a bread crust, and tied in for the last long carry of nine miles. Up and down, rocks, fallen trees and mud holes, brush and briers, slippery corduroys and slimy logs. It was a wearisome carry, but I made it. I had started at 5 a.m.; I sighted the Tannery at 1:30 p.m.

Declining the offer of a friend to "set" me across, I took out, launched, and ferried myself over, landed in the Tannery ooze, drew the Sairy up into the fresh, green grass, wiped her frail siding clean and "tied in" neatly and carefully. Then, amid the questions and congratulations of a dozen good-natured friends, I mounted her on my head for a last short carry to the hotel and walked wearily up to the hospitable door of the Moose River House. I laid her down carefully on the shady porch, as a mother would a tired infant, and the cruise of the *Sairy Gamp* was ended.

I have little more to add. I had cruised her, by paddle and carry, 118 miles on the outward trip, and, by a different route, 148 miles on the return. She had been a surprise to me. It required care and caution to get into or out of such a light, limber boat. But, once seated fairly, she was steady as a whole-boat. Her builder thought her too small and light for a working boat. He was a trifle mistaken. I would as soon take her to float a deer or handle a large fish as any canoe I have ever owned; but her carrying capacity is, of course, small. She "trims" best at 140 pounds. Say 110 pounds at the seat and fifteen pounds at each stem.

At another time and place I shall have more to say on the open canoe and double-blade. But my outing is over for this year. I have brought the *Sairy* home without a check in her frail siding. She sits lightly on a shelf, where I can rest my eyes on her, as

> I turn and raise the load,
> With weary shoulders bending;
> And take the old, well-beaten road,
> That leads—unto the ending.
>   NESSMUK

P.S.—To the oft-recurring question of my friends, "What luck fishing and hunting?" I answer I have not been fishing and hunting. I fished a little, incidentally; hunted not at all. To those who assume that I have been straggling and cruising through the Northern Wilderness for six weeks, that I may say I have cruised the lightest working cedar canoe ever built, I can only say they are badly mistaken. I don't know that she is the lightest, and there are scores of canoeists who can handle her as well or better than her present owner. The few who call me a "canoe crank" and "hobby rider" come nearer the mark. I think myself it is a hobby— but a mighty pleasant one to ride.

                                                      N.

The editor of *Forest and Stream* added the following postscript to the above letter:

Mr. Rushton sends us a letter received from "Nessmuk" from which we quote: "To-day I send you back the *Sairy Gamp*. She is of no further use to me. There is not a lake in Tioga County, and I am not going to rattle her over the stones of Pine Creek. She has astonished me; she will be more of a surprise to you. Remember the advice you gave me about bracing, etc. Remember you said you 'would not warrant her for an hour; she may go to pieces like an eggshell.' That's what you said; she don't go to pieces worth a cent. I have snagged her, rocked her, got her onto spruce knots, and been rattled down rapids stern foremost; and I send her back, as tight and staunch as the day I took her at Boonville. There are more than a hundred cuts, scratches, and abrasions on her thin siding, there are red and green blotches on her strips, from contact with amateur boats, and longer streaks of blue from collisions, with the regulation guide boat, but she does not leak a drop. I once said in *Forest and Stream* I was trying to find out how light a canoe it took to drown a man. I never shall know. The *Sairy Gamp* has only ducked me once in a six weeks' cruise, and that by my own carelessness."